THERE SHOULD HAVE BEEN FIVE

MJ Honikman

Tafelberg

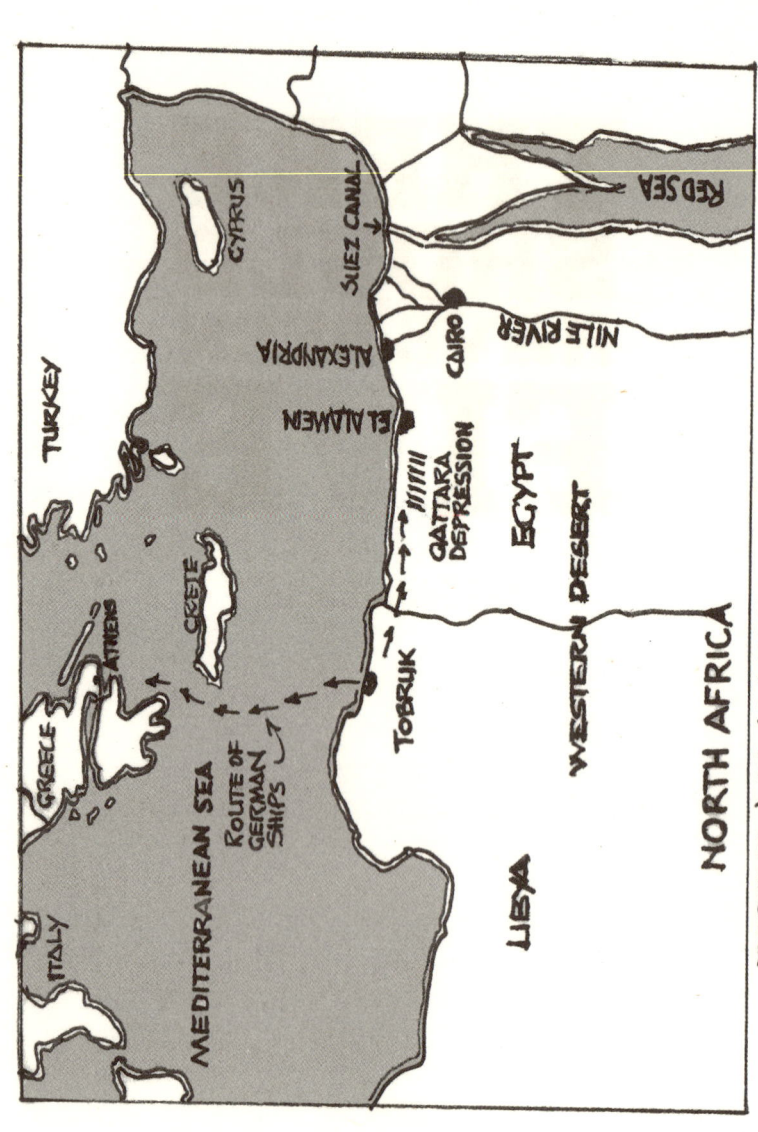

TOBRUK & EL ALAMEIN – JULY 1942

This is for the great-grandchildren of the 354 000 South Africans of all races who volunteered to serve in South Africa's defence force and nursing services in the fight against Hitler, the Nazis and the Italian fascists in World War II.

First published in 2016 by Tafelberg,
an imprint of NB Publishers,
a division of Media24 Boeke (Pty) Ltd,
40 Heerengracht, Cape Town
Text © 2016 M.J. Honikman
Typographic design and setting by Chérie Collins
Maps by Richard Honikman
Photographs courtesy of Ditsong: National Museum of Military History
Cover photograph of POWs by Josie Borain

Printed by *paarlmedia*, a division of Novus Holdings

First edition, first impression 2016

ISBN: 978-0-624-07656-8
E-PUB: 978-0-624-07657-5
MOBI: 978-0-624-07658-2

All rights reserved.

No part of this book may be reproduced or transmitted in any form or by any electronic or mechanical means, including photocopying and recording, or by any other storage or retrieval system, without written permission from the publisher.

"What did you do in the war, Daddy?" my big brother would ask, and our father would tell us about his adventures, not about the fighting. We heard how an unarmed and very young black soldier saved his life in the mountains of Abyssinia. I have used the anecdotes our father told us about this brave man to develop the character Sipho Ndebele, through whose eyes much of this story is told.

1
Counting minutes

Tobruk Harbour, Libya, North Africa
July 1942

Sipho had been edgy all day. He wasn't sure what was going to happen on the ship, but he knew it would be dangerous, it would be soon, and that somehow he would have to help.

A crane swung the last load of petrol drums across the deck towards him. Sipho reached up to the heavy rope net, positioned it over the hatch, and then watched as it dropped into the hold where Job was waiting.

Sipho was moving away from the open hatch, his back foot still in the air, when the ship lurched. He was pitched forward, bruising his palms as he grabbed at the hatch's upturned lip, which saved him from plummeting head first into the hold.

In the gloom below he saw Job loosen the net, free a petrol drum and roll it past boxes of ammunition to the back of the hold, where two men wrestled the drum upright and shoved it against several hundred others that were already stashed there. Sipho sat back on his haunches with a grunt, relieved to be alive and relieved, he realised, that Job hadn't seen him stumble.

He's not sure I'm up to this, Sipho thought. *Will he always think of me as Mzi's little brother?*

He rubbed his aching hands against his thighs and stood, stretching his gaunt body to its full height and noticing, with wry satisfaction, little knots of muscle on his wiry biceps after all the weeks of backbreaking work.

I know I'm up to it. I must be eighteen by now – I've been in the army for nearly a year.

He breathed deeply and swallowed the bile burning the back of his throat.

The ship righted itself and then lurched heavily again. He heard a thump behind him and the ship juddered.

This is it! It's started! He whipped around and saw the swell that had pushed in through the harbour mouth, bumping the ship against the barge tied up alongside.

It hadn't started, but the sun was dipping low towards the dusty hills.

Any minute now . . .

*

Early that morning, before they'd left the prison camp, Lance Corporal Job Maseko had beckoned to Sipho, his friend Andrew and three other prisoners of war to gather close. Standing a head taller than any of them, Job had spoken quietly in isiZulu.

"Ngizwe kahle. Listen carefully. We don't have to give up just because we're POWs. The Nazis must not win this war. There's something we can do today. On the ship."

Sipho had been dubious. "What can we do," he'd wondered aloud, "with an Italian guard watching us every minute?"

Job had looked at each of them in turn, with a glimmer of a smile and a glint of defiance, although he'd hesitated as he'd caught Sipho's eye.

"Last thing this afternoon, just before we leave the ship, find a way to get the guard to look away, out to sea. Franco's our guard today. He's just a kid, not much older than you, Sipho, and he likes to fool about. It'll be easy to distract him. I need you guys to keep him busy for a few minutes. Andrew, do something to get his attention. The rest of you, help Andrew. And don't ask why! The less I tell you, the safer you'll be."

Andrew, sturdy and unruffled, had given Job a slight grin. Round-eyed, the other men had nodded silently.

Sipho usually kept away from the Italian guards. Most were unfriendly and some were vicious – a few days before, a guard had shot dead a prisoner of war who'd been slow to obey an order. Since then, Sipho had experienced a growing numbness as he made it through each day, trying not to think too far into the future – a future which seemed darkly unknowable.

And now Sipho knew Job was expecting them to risk their lives, but he'd nodded along with the others.

He would not say no to Job.

Now, in the late afternoon on a lurching ship, Sipho snuck an anxious glance at the guard. Job was right: Franco did look young to be a guard and he seemed quite friendly.

But Italian guards were unpredictable.

*

Franco had spent a long, lonely day guarding the South African prisoners of war.

He had watched them roll petrol drums from the dock onto a flat barge that then chugged out to the ship, and he'd watched them manoeuvre the drums into a net so the ship's crane could hoist them up and lower them into the hold.

The work was heavy, the day airless and the heat fierce, but the prisoners had been in good spirits, with the tallest prisoner of war, the one they called Job, singing as he worked and the others chanting the chorus. Franco had been a little envious, almost wishing he could join them. But he had strict instructions, so he'd tried to look stern as he stood with his feet apart and arms folded, until the petrol drums were on board, the hatch closed for the night and he could relax in the light breeze that now wafted in from the sea.

He leant against the ship's rail, his rifle propped next to him, and lazily watched the prisoners packing away the equipment. One of the men, the sturdy one, shoved a net into its box and gave a jaunty swagger.

"Can you dance, Franco? Can you dance like us?"

*

Sipho sucked in his breath. Andrew! Was he crazy, being sassy to an Italian guard? Sipho waited for Franco to react; the other prisoners of war watching silently.

Would Franco understand the English words, or would he only hear the provocative tone? The ropes in the men's hands dropped to the deck and they stood frozen, expectant.

A slow smile lit up Franco's face.

"In South Africa, we dance! We'll teach you!" someone called out to him.

Andrew lifted a bent leg to his shoulder. "Like this, Franco!"

Andrew stamped down with a double beat, thud-THUD and then again, thud-thud, pause, thud-THUD. A few men started singing, swaying in time. With a laugh, Franco slicked back his dark hair, stamped his foot and moved away from the rail. Andrew shimmied behind Franco, jostling him with his elbows to face the harbour mouth, the gap between the surrounding hills.

Franco tried to copy their dance with a few wild kicks, and then he laughed at his own poor efforts. He gave up on the high kicks and, spreading his arms wide, stamped his heels to the same double beat. He stepped forward and across, thud-THUD, and back again.

"I too can dance!" Franco said to Andrew. "I dance like the Greek men. My papou, my grandfather he is Greek." Franco seemed hardly to move. Just his heels beat down as his body rotated slowly.

Sipho looked around uneasily, wondering where Job was. He'd seen two men come out of the hatch and close it carefully for the night. So where was Job? It was usually easy to spot him: a tall man with striking looks, high cheekbones and an aquiline nose. But Job was not with the dancers. He was nowhere on the deck.

Sipho stood still, wondering how he was supposed to help. Andrew caught his eye and flicked his head towards three men dancing in front of the hatch, one of whom, a bit older than the others, called out through the clamour of singing, "Ndebele! Woza! Come join us here, Sipho!" He reached out a hand, clasped Sipho's arm and pulled him towards the group so they could pack close.

So Sipho danced, crouching low and kicking high.

Franco slowly swivelled, stamping his heels and looking at each of the dancing men, and then at the men coiling the last of the ropes. His glance slid to Sipho's tight group in front of the hatch, and for a second he paused. His eyes focused, through their legs, on the closed hatch and then he shifted round towards the open sea.

While Franco's back was turned, Sipho scanned the length of the ship, searching again for Job.

Has Franco noticed Job is missing?

But Franco was looking out at where the breeze blew shadows across the bright water, and dancing with the beat until a prisoner of war knocked his heel against Franco's rifle. It slipped sideways, and another prisoner of war made a grab to save it from dropping overboard. Franco panicked. *Was he mad? Fraternising with POWs?*

He snatched back his rifle and stood at attention. In an instant he changed back into a guard, and they were all just prisoners of war once more.

"Fall into line!" Franco ordered. "On to the barge! March!" And he led the way down the gangplank.

Someone nudged Sipho's elbow and there was Job grinning at him, with that glint, again, in his eye.

"Time to go and watch a strange sunset, Sipho," Job said.

The prisoners of war filed down the gangplank to the flat barge where Franco was waiting. As Job stepped on to the barge, Franco's eyes were watching him thoughtfully, and Sipho's stomach cramped. What did Franco know? But Job stood with his feet wide apart, balancing confidently as they rode the swells towards the dock.

By the time the barge bumped against rubber tyres on the

quay, Sipho's fingers were numb from gripping the rail, his back tense as he kept it braced, expecting for endless moments a blast behind him. At the dock, the prisoners jumped ashore and swung up onto the open lorry waiting on the wharf. No one looked back at the ship.

But there was none of the usual talk as the lorry jolted through the bombed and burnt-out warehouses and lumbered up the stony road from the harbour to the prisoner-of-war camp in the desert. Job sat back, but Sipho and the other men were quiet and tense, hugging their knees and listening, waiting. They knew an explosion would bring a visit from the grim-faced military police. And who of them would survive such a visit? Would Job?

Sipho found himself counting seconds, and then minutes, the way he had done down in the gold mine when a fuse was lit. Why was it was taking so long? Something should have happened already. The desert dust boiled up beneath the lorry's wheels, stinging the men's eyes and clogging their nostrils.

Sipho did not notice.

He counted as the minutes stretched out, and he longed for the quiet hills of his home.

What had brought him here? It was Job, of course, the city boy who had visited their remote valley every summer for as long as he could remember, bringing his lightness with him. Job had always seemed fearless, Sipho thought, wishing he was too.

I've been scared every day and every night since we left South Africa, he realised. Bombs, shells, a lion and a hyena in Abyssinia were bad enough. But people – the Askaris in Abyssinia, the guards and the military police here – they frighten me the most. And maybe I've always been afraid.

Pictures from his childhood slipped through his mind as minutes passed. A vivid image appeared suddenly. He was a small boy in a calf pen and he was frozen with fear.

Job had been watching, he remembered.

2

A letter from the mine

South Africa, 1930s

Sipho's father set up his milking stool beside a white cow with a spattering of brown spots across its back. "Sipho! Bring this cow's calf to me!"

Sipho's older brother, Mzi, was watching with a friend, a tall boy from the city, who was visiting his grandparents down the valley.

Sipho had never fetched a calf from the pen before. He sidled through the gate into the calf pen and closed it carefully. The calves were a head taller than him. They surged towards him, bumping and shoving hard against his ribs. He battled to keep his balance. The biggest calf licked at his neck with a long, urgent tongue, hoping to find something to suckle. Sipho stood rigid with fear. He was sure Mzi had never been afraid of calves.

"Baba!" he tried to yell to his father. "I can't!" He opened his mouth and no sound came out.

Across the pen, he saw a white calf with a few brown spots – the calf his father needed.

Mzi thinks I can do this, he thought and he made his eyes focus only on that calf as he pushed through the others. When he got to it, he wrapped his arms around the calf's neck and tugged it out of the pen to where his father sat, ready to milk the cow.

Sipho positioned the calf so that it could suckle for a few minutes on the cow's richest milk, and then he heaved the reluctant calf away, so that his father could milk into the bucket. And he went to fetch the next calf.

His father murmured approval. His mother, who had stopped to watch, continued on her way into their homestead. Mzi and his tall friend both nodded, and the friend gave a cheerful wave with two stout sticks he was holding. Sipho glowed.

Later that day Sipho saw the tall boy using those same sticks to fight Mzi. Holding his own two sticks, Mzi was being beaten down the hill. Sipho ran towards them. He shouted in alarm and the two boys collapsed onto the grass, rocking with laughter. Sipho started to walk away, stiff with embarrassment.

"See if you can beat me, Sipho! Your brother can't," the tall boy called out to him with a wide grin. "Mzi, give him your sticks."

"Here, Sipho!" Laughing, Mzi handed him the sticks. "You have to beat Job! Our family honour is at stake."

Sipho waved the heavy sticks wildly at Job.

"That's fine if you're shooing flies, Sipho, but if you want to stick fight, hold this stick in the middle to fend me off, like this, and hold the other stick near the bottom to use as a weapon, like that."

Sipho knew Job pretended to lose that fight, but he thought his heart would burst with pride. Until he saw his father shaking his head as he walked away.

"Our father thinks fighting's stupid," Mzi explained to Job. "He says we should sort things by talking. Our uncles think he's soft in the head."

Job had thought about this for a moment, and then gathered up the sticks and tucked them under his arm. "Maybe he's not so soft in the head."

When Mzi grew up he left home to work in a coal mine. Each Christmas he came home with a suitcase of presents. One year a letter came from the manager of the coal mine. Sipho's father brought the letter home from the trading store, and handed it to Sipho. Sipho's mother stood close.

"Read the letter, Sipho!" his father said.

Sipho opened the envelope and took out a single page and six five-pound notes. The ground heaved under his feet as he read the mine manager's words.

*

Years later, on a summer afternoon, Sipho trudged slowly along a well-worn track through the veld. He wore Mzi's jacket, which hung loose and baggy on his lanky frame. He walked with his head down and his shoulders hunched and he sighed as he looked at his bare feet.

I hope my children will have shoes to wear to my funeral.

Life had been so hard for them all, for so long. And now he had no one. Why, he wondered, was he thinking about shoes?

Behind him two mounds lay side by side on the hillside. His mother's was covered in thick, green veld-grass, his father's in raw earth. There was no mound for Mzi, who had died years before in a coal-mine fire.

There were no bodies. The fire burnt for three days, the mine manager had written in that pitiful letter.

"Thirty pounds for my son's life! Sipho, promise me you will never work in a coal mine," his grief-stricken mother had wailed.

After Mzi's death she no longer sang as she worked. She'd gone to her thatch-roofed rondavel early every afternoon and lain on a grass mat. One day she couldn't get up. Sipho's father had thought she was dying of grief and anger. He'd laid her in the back of an ox-drawn cart and taken her over the hills to the mission hospital. The doctor had told him she had cancer and gave her a packet of painkillers. There was nothing they could do, he'd said.

So Sipho's father had brought her home and she'd sunk back onto her grass mat.

Sipho had crouched next to her with a bowl of imasi, holding out a spoonful of the creamy curds. She had shaken her head and then, seeing his bleak look, patted his hand and murmured, "You're growing to be a good, strong man like your brother was."

But Mzi seemed to do most things effortlessly.

She'd sensed his thought and her voice was not much more than a sigh. "Perhaps you don't know it, but I do."

When she died the whole world seemed to mourn her. The winds that usually brought rain to the valley brought high, wispy clouds and then turned and blew the other way. There was no rain in the valley for two summers. Dry winds sent wildfires roaring over the hills and a dull haze of smoke and dust hung in the sky. The mealie plants grew knee-high and then withered. The grass that survived the fires did not make seed heads. Streams dried and cattle got thin, limping and foaming at the mouth.

On a hot, windy day two men from the government rode up on horseback. One of the men had been before. He was the extension officer who had persuaded all the farmers, black and white, on both sides of the great river, to dip their cattle to kill ticks, and to plough around the hill so summer storms did not wash away the topsoil. Sipho's father knew and trusted him. The other man was a vet. The two men opened their saddle bags, took out white coats and long rubber gloves, and examined the sick animals.

Sipho heard the vet tell his father he would have to kill all his cattle.

Sipho's father stared at him in disbelief.

"And burn the carcases. You cannot eat the meat or you'll get ill. This is foot and mouth disease. We must stay and watch the cattle burn," the vet had added.

Sipho's father was angry. Just a few months earlier the government had taken good land from black farmers in other parts of the country. "Is this because we are black farmers? Does the government want to take our land now too?"

The extension officer put a hand on his shoulder. "Ndebele, this terrible disease does not notice colour. This is the only way to stop it – there is no medicine for it. Across the river we did the same. Some of the white farmers can't pay what they owe the banks, and the banks have taken their farms. Those farmers have gone to Johannesburg to look for work."

When the two men rode away the smell of burning bones and horns lingered in the valley, even inside the rondavels. Sipho's father and his uncles, all the farmers in the valley, who had husbanded their abundant herds so well, and whose fat Nguni cattle had once dotted the hillsides, were left with nothing.

And then Sipho's father had started to cough.

*

Leaving the graves, Sipho walked slowly to the homestead. His feet grew heavy and, when he reached the fence of prickly pear bushes, he stood at the opening and looked at his father's empty rondavel. It had been so sudden. Two days ago the cough had got worse. By evening his father had struggled to breathe and then, just before dawn, his breathing had slowed and stopped.

Mzi. His mother. His father.

He had no one left.

His half-uncles were not friendly. And all Sipho had were empty grasslands. How would he find food? What could he do? When he tried to think about the future his mind slipped sideways. He wished he had not politely taken a sip of sorghum beer each time his uncle's wife had passed the calabash his way.

He shook his head to clear it and slumped on a grass mat in the shade of a small tree near his rondavel.

It was late afternoon and, although the sun had not yet set, the daylight seemed dim. From a copse of trees next to the stream he heard a piet-my-vrou call, "Phezu komkhono, it's time to hoe your land." He lifted his head and gave a half smile. His mother had loved that call. "Early summer and my hoeing must get done. I must get the mealie seeds into the ground," she would say. This summer the rains had come but he had no mealie seeds to plant.

But from the hilltop now there seemed to come another call.
"Sipho! Woza! Come! Sipho!"
And "Woza . . . Sipho . . . Sipho . . . " echoing off the opposite hills.

3

A photograph of a man with a little black moustache

Sipho saw a tall, broad-shouldered figure silhouetted against the sky.

The man seemed to survey the whole valley and then he waved at Sipho and, when Sipho did not get up, came striding down the hill towards him. He was dressed in an open overcoat, much too hot for a summer's day, and he carried a large suitcase on his shoulder. He sprang lightly over the grass and into the yard as if the suitcase was weightless.

It was Job.

The dim sky seemed to brighten.

Sipho sat up straight. "Job! You're back! Sawubona! Unjani? I'm pleased to see you!"

Job swung the suitcase from his shoulder and plonked himself down on the grass mat next to Sipho. "Yebo! Back to see my grandparents. I need a drink of water, Sipho," Job said.

Sipho dipped a calabash into a large clay pot and handed it to Job.

"You're wearing a smart coat!" Sipho felt foolish speaking about such a thing when his father had just been buried.

"Yes! For my grandfather. For next winter. It's too warm for this weather," Job laughed, "but it's easier to wear it than carry it. And for you . . ." He opened his suitcase. "Here's a blanket for you and one for your father. The others are for my grandparents."

He pulled out two thick blankets and Sipho had to turn his head away and take a breath before he could speak. "Job, we buried my father today. I've just come from the funeral."

"Hhayi bo! No! Sipho, I'm sorry! I thought the summer would fix your father's cough."

"He would not go to the hospital."

They sat quietly.

"You must go and see your grandparents, Job," Sipho said at last.

Job lifted the suitcase on to his shoulder, saying mildly as he went on his way, "We'll talk tomorrow . . . about your plans. Keep both blankets."

The sun had set but Sipho sat a while longer.

Job would help him make a plan, just as he had helped before.

*

Job visited his grandparents at Christmas every year, spending long summer days in the lush Natal hills. Job and Mzi made a bow and a few arrows for Sipho and taught him to hunt field mice in the long grass, and dassies amongst the rocks. Up on the hills, when Sipho was watching cattle, they would practise stick fighting or splash under small waterfalls.

At the end of one of these visits, in the days when Mzi and his mother were alive, when the cattle were fat and life was good,

Job had said to Sipho, "Before I go, I want to talk to your father."

Sipho had seen Job walk up to the dip tank, where his father had nearly finished dipping the cattle.

When Sipho's father had noticed Job and nodded, Job had greeted him respectfully.

"Sawubona, Baba." He'd paused. "Baba, there's a school now, over the hill. Have you thought of letting Sipho learn to read?"

Sipho's father had swung his long whip over his head. It had cracked like a gunshot. He'd silently watched the last cow jump into the soupy water, swim the length of the dip tank and stumble up the ramp. Job had waited. Sipho's father then folded the whip, tucked it under his arm and turned to look silently at Job.

"School," he'd said at last. "I did not go to school. There is nothing wrong with me. See how many cows I have. See how many cows have calves. I am a wealthy man. Sipho does not need to read. Mzi cannot read and he has good work at the coal mine. He sends us money every month. Why would Sipho need to go to school?"

In those days it was unheard of for a young man to contradict an older man. Job did so with such grace that Sipho's father hardly noticed. They walked back to the homestead and Job asked if he knew how Mzi was getting on at the mine in Welkom. He wondered if they had heard any news. When Sipho's father shook his head, Job said, "At the school they will also teach Sipho to write. He can write a letter to Mzi and ask how he is."

Sipho's father had not looked impressed. "But will the letter come back?" he wanted to know.

For a minute Job was puzzled. "Do you mean will a reply come back?" he asked. "Sipho can say in the letter that Mzi should find someone to write a letter to you, with his news."

Sipho's father had stood still for a minute and then given a quick nod.

*

Just before the sun rose on the first day of term, Sipho was already walking up the hill to the school that lay far down the next valley, near the great river. He was big to be starting school, almost in his teens. His feet were heavy and slow. He was not sure what a school was, but when people spoke of someone who had been to school there was a tone in their voices that made him think school was important, so he did not tell anyone he was nervous.

He reached the crest of the hill and then his feet refused to move. He turned to look back the way he had come. It was nearly milking time, and on every side of the wide valley young boys were driving herds of cattle down from the grazing land behind their homesteads. But behind his home a grown man was driving the herd. His father.

His father's half-brothers thought it was foolish for a grown man to spend his days looking after cattle when he had a son who could do it. Sipho knew they would say so and make his father feel bad.

His hands were clammy with shame for his father, and with worry about what lay in the next valley, but then he breathed deeply, turned his back on the sight of his father doing boys' work and hurried down to the distant small building.

*

The school was run by Miss Jabulani and an Irish nun, Sister Katherine. Miss Jabulani spoke isiZulu to her class, but Sister Katherine spoke only English. Sipho was put in Sister Katherine's class with the big children. For the first nine weeks he sat in complete silence. He did not understand a word she said until one day, when some of the sounds started to mean something. A week later he spoke a full sentence of English.

After the winter holiday Sister Katherine brought a newspaper back from the city. On the front page was a photograph of a black man being presented with a medal.

"The fastest man in the world," she told them. "Jessie Owens. He won four gold medals at the Olympic Games in Germany. And this man . . . " She pointed to a photograph of a dark-haired man with a little black moustache. "This man, the German ruler, was very put out, very cross, because Jessie Owens is black. This is Adolf Hitler. He doesn't like Jewish people and he doesn't like black people. A cruel man, this! A dangerous man! And he wants to rule the world."

Sipho asked if he could take the newspaper to show his father the picture of a black man winning a gold medal. Sipho's father was more interested in hearing about Adolf Hitler.

After two years, Sister Katherine gave Sipho paper and an envelope and he painstakingly wrote a letter to Mzi. He ran over the far hills to Mr Aaron's trading store to post it.

Mr Aaron spoke fluent isiZulu and sometimes, when Sipho's father took his dried cow skins to sell to Mr Aaron, they talked about the worrying news from Germany.

Mrs Aaron was gentle and quiet-spoken. She had a long table in a back room where women customers could cut panels of blue seshoeshoe cloth and sew them into skirts on her treadle sewing machine.

Mrs Aaron was alone in the store when Sipho got there. He produced the envelope and took a copper penny from his pocket.

"Here's a stamp, Sipho." She pointed at the leather post bag. "Drop your letter in the bag. Mr Aaron is loading the lorry now. He'll be taking the post today."

When a reply arrived at the trading store, Sipho's father brought it home.

"Mr Aaron said he could read it to me. But I told him, thank you but my son, Sipho, can read it."

So Sipho read the letter to his parents.

When he had finished, his father said, "Good! Sipho can write a letter, and the letter comes back. It's time for him to look after the cattle again."

With that, Sipho's schooling came to an end.

But Sister Katherine asked Sipho if he would like to come once a week to fetch her old newspapers. "I think your father likes to know the news, Sipho."

So for several years Sipho ran over the hill each Friday to fetch the newspapers. His father heard what was happening in the world, and Sipho did not forget how to read.

*

The army lorry braked and Sipho pitched against the man next to him. His face scraped against a rough army uniform as he came out of his reverie.

They were at the prisoner-of-war camp.

Sipho climbed off the lorry onto spiky desert scrub so different from the misty grasslands he had left.

He knew that if he had stayed, if he had not taken Job's advice, he would probably have starved in his beautiful hills.

4

To the city

Early in the morning the day after the funeral, Job had appeared at Sipho's rondavel with an enamel bowl of imasi heaped with ground amabele grain. He pulled a woven-grass mat out into the sunlight and sat next to Sipho.

"Here, eat. From my grandmother," Job said. "She got a shock when she saw you at the funeral. Said you were just big eyes in a skinny face." He paused. "I don't see anything for you here, Sipho. So what are you going to do?"

Sipho waved a spoon at the vivid green veld around his kraal. "I have lots of grass this summer but no animals to graze it, and no mealie seeds to plant. Our crops died two summers in a row. There is nothing here for me, Job."

"Do you have any food at all?" Job asked.

Sipho pointed to a sack of mealiemeal and a big tin of powdered milk under the thatched eaves behind him. "I just saw these a few minutes ago. From the trading store. Enough for a few weeks. And there's a note." He read it to Job.

"*Dear Sipho, We were sorry to hear of your father's death. He was a fine man. Mrs Aaron joins me in wishing you a long life. Joshua Aaron.*"

Job nodded. "They liked your father."

"My father liked them." Sipho took a spoonful of the creamy curds and nutty amabele. "I haven't had time," he added slowly, "to think what I will do. My uncles have nothing left either. No cows . . . Their sons are going to work in the coal mine, but I promised my mother I wouldn't."

"Your uncles!" Job stretched out his legs and laughed wryly. "They mocked your father for watching the cattle so you could go to school. Don't count on them!" He pointed at a hill, far down the valley, where two cows grazed.

"See there? I sent money to my grandfather so he could buy those two cows. Sipho, did your mother say anything about gold mines?" he asked.

Sipho shook his head.

"You know South Africa is fighting a war?"

Sipho nodded. "Against Hitler. Against Germany."

"And Italy," Job added. "The Nazis and the fascists."

"My father thought Jan Smuts was right to fight Hitler. Because Hitler's not a man you can talk to."

"I agree," Job said. "But now so many miners are going away to fight that the mines are looking for men. I work at the mine, and sometimes at the dynamite factory, but I stay there at the mine. Come back with me. They will listen to your heart and, if it is strong, if it beats slowly, you can work underground."

"Am I old enough?" Sipho asked.

"You're quite tall. Are you eighteen?"

Sipho shook his head, a little embarrassed. "I don't know. Maybe sixteen, maybe nearly seventeen."

"I know plenty of miners who don't know how old they are,"

Job said confidently. "And perhaps the mine bosses won't ask. The mine is dangerous, it's dark and too hot, and the food is bad. But you need not stay long. Save your money to buy a couple of cows and you can come home in a year. I'm going back after Christmas. Think about it."

*

And so, on a night in January 1941, Sipho sat on a hard bench next to a sleeping Job as their train steamed through bright lights into a town. The brakes screeched, the coaches clanged together and men shouted. A large white board appeared on a platform.

"SPRINGS," Sipho read.

Job awoke and he led Sipho through the streets of a strange world. There were men who seemed angry for no reason, and policemen with batons, and other men who looked fearful. Job and Sipho walked out of the town until they reached a large gate in front of the grim compound of a gold mine. Silhouetted against the moonlit sky was a tall metal structure with a large wheel, higher than anything Sipho had ever seen, and with red lights that seemed to float above it. Under his feet, the ground felt unsteady as he gazed up.

"Just until you can buy some cows," Job reassured him. "If you know it's not forever, it's easier. They will check your heart and lungs in the morning and then sign you on."

Job showed his pass to the mine policeman at the gate and told him who Sipho was. Inside the compound they entered a long room where a light shone through high steel windows onto twenty concrete bunks, and eighteen sleeping men. The men did not stir as Sipho and Job found the empty bunks. Dirty clothes were piled on the floor next to the bunks; Sipho saw that there was nowhere else to put them.

Wrapping his blankets around himself that strange night, he lay awake on the bare concrete bunk, listening to snores and grunts and a high whistling, whirring sound from outside. All night he worried – *Will I be able to do this work so deep underground? What will it be like down there in the dark?* – until at dawn a bell clanged.

Sipho trained at the mine school for a week. At one point a man from the dynamite factory came to give the new miners a lesson. Job came into the room with him and translated the lesson from English into Funagalo, the strange language they spoke on the mine. Sipho listened, amazed; Job spoke such beautiful isiZulu, and this language was like that of a small child.

In Funagalo, Job told them, "You will not be working with dynamite but, because it is so dangerous, you must know something about it. We don't ever hurry with dynamite. We get things ready and then we work calmly."

The instructor showed them what a fuse wire was, and how long it needed to be, and he told them they would all need to stand far away, near the shaft, before the fuse wire was lit and the dynamite exploded. Sipho looked anxiously at the fuse wire as if to memorise its length.

A week later, Sipho became a trammer.

On his first day of work, he entered the mine lift with thirty other new recruits, all wide-eyed. A few were hyperventilating. The lift dropped deep into the earth's crust, and travelled for nearly twenty minutes to reach the level where he would work. He had expected to be afraid, but, when the lift opened, he stepped calmly out into a thick, woolly blackness, although the heat made his head ache. The lamp on his helmet made a small pool of light: Sipho could see where to put his feet, but nothing else unless he lifted his head. He spent the day loading loose rocks on to a tram, which he had to push to the mine shaft and then back, filling it again and again. He was so tired at the end of the ten-hour shift that he fell deeply asleep as soon as he dropped onto the concrete bunk.

The heat, the dark and the dust underground were grim, but Sipho thought he could get used to that.

I won't ever get used to the izinduna taunting us with their sjamboks, he thought, *or the food that is sour, or the dirty rooms we sleep in. A whole year of this before I can get home?*

The explosions terrified him, so he always made sure he was well away from the fuse wires when they were lit, and he counted the seconds before the dynamite exploded. The blast seemed to suck the air out of his lungs, and dust filled them when he breathed again.

Some of the mineworkers spent their Sundays drinking sorghum beer in the shacks behind the mine. Sipho heard piano music and a woman singing in English, a song about a train. As the months passed, Sipho thought of joining them; it might make life feel easier.

"Oh no, not me!" Job told him. "Those guys will have to come back next year because their money will be gone. Stick it out, Sipho, and save your money to buy your cows! The cows will be your bank."

The next week Job returned to work at the dynamite factory, translating for the trainer. One night he spoke quietly to Sipho.

"I've met quite a woman, Sipho!" he said dreamily. "There, at the dynamite factory. She works in the office. Zanele . . . " Job seemed to savour the sound of her name. "Her family comes from a valley near ours. She is clever and beautiful, and she has a lovely laugh. I think she likes me. But the lobola! They will want a lot of cows for the bride price . . . "

5

General Smuts makes a promise

"Still not enough for lobola, Sipho."

It was a warm Sunday afternoon a few months after Sipho had started working, and the mine was quiet. Sipho watched as Job paged through his post office book, counting up his savings. Job sat on an empty paraffin can out in the sun, while Sipho sharpened a long-handled razor.

"Cut it short. I like the parting on the left," Job instructed.

Sipho carefully shaved a straight, narrow parting through Job's hair, thinking while he did so that he had never known Job to trouble himself so much over a woman.

"Anyone would think you had somewhere special to go . . . like a dynamite factory," Sipho said.

Job smiled but kept his head still while Sipho trimmed the edges.

Many of the miners had gone to a dance competition and their buses were shortly due to return, so Sipho and Job did not look up when they heard the rumble of a large motor vehicle coming into the compound. They did look up when, instead of loud laughter and talking, they heard quiet murmuring.

Three men in khaki uniforms climbed out of an army lorry.

They set up a table and three folding chairs, and were already sitting at the table when the buses did return.

"Gather around!" one of the men called through the megaphone as the miners milled around. "We have news that will interest you all," he said.

The man told them their country needed them to join the army to fight Hitler.

"We have contracts with the mine!" one of the miners shouted. "You're wasting your time. We aren't allowed to leave the mine till our contracts are up. And anyway, what has our country done for us black men?" he asked.

"Your country will help you now. You will be trained. You will be taught new skills, to drive lorries or ambulances, and to fix them, or to be medical orderlies. And you will be well paid, better than here," the man in uniform replied. And as an afterthought: "The mine is not allowed to keep anyone who wants to join the army. The Italian army is helping Germany. They have invaded countries in East Africa and they are threatening to take over the Union of South Africa. Our army is fighting with the Allies to stop them. Join the army now, and you will travel to interesting places! You will see the world! You will have wonderful stories to tell your children and your grandchildren!"

Many of the men drifted away, muttering about risking their lives for a country that did not care about them. Job stepped closer to where a group of miners had gathered around the table.

"How much will you pay?" he asked the army officers.

The man in uniform gave him a leaflet with the pay rates. "We'll be back next Sunday," the man told him as he folded his chair.

*

"*Buy a few good clothes and save the rest.*" Sipho reflected on Job's advice as he sat in the sun-drenched compound the following Sunday. "*Don't spend yet! Wait a bit before you have fun, till you've saved enough money.*"

Piano notes floated from somewhere over the wall, and the thrum of a double bass.

Sipho was torn. His didn't have enough money yet to buy a cow, but life in the compound was grim. Beyond the wall he could hear people laughing, and he was about to go and look for the piano when a large car drove, spluttering, into the compound.

The driver left the engine running as he climbed out and lifted the bonnet, and Sipho wandered over to watch. The driver took out a screwdriver and fiddled with something, and the engine raced loudly. He worked under the bonnet some more, until it hummed sweetly.

To Sipho, it seemed to sing. And he knew instantly that he would save his money, but that he would not use it to buy cows – this is what he wanted, a motor car.

Job was suddenly in front of him, flapping a newspaper.

"Sipho! News! Two bits of news! Here's the first, on the front page of *The Star*." Job pointed to a photograph of Jan Smuts.

Sipho nodded. "The Prime Minister."

Job sat down next to Sipho as other miners looked up. "See what he said . . . " Job started reading from the newspaper headline. "*At the Premier Mine Training Camp yesterday General Smuts told trainee soldiers they would be fighting for freedom.*"

A couple more men came over and peered at the photograph.

Job continued, " . . . *we now go forth . . . to fight for freedom itself, the freedom of the human spirit, the free choice of the human individual to shape his own life . . . The world cause of freedom is also our cause and we shall wage this war for human freedom . . .* "

"Heybo! Promises, promises!" said one man as some others laughed. "You think the abelungu will keep their promises? And that Jan Smuts? Slim Jannie! He's too clever, and slippery."

"But see this!" Job insisted, pointing at another article. "The Nazis are putting Jewish people on trains and no one knows what happens to them. They just disappear!"

Sipho thought with dismay of Mr Aaron. *Does he have family in Germany?*

He reached out, took *The Star* from Job and read on.

Another man called out loudly, "Why should we worry about the Jews?"

"Because one day it might be you!" a usually quiet man said firmly.

"It could be you. Hitler doesn't like black people either," Job spoke out. "I read that there are not many black people left in Germany. Some have escaped and many have been killed. A few black actors have been allowed to stay for Nazi propaganda films, to act as buffoons, and they have been sterilised so they can't have children."

There was a horrified silence.

"So what will he do if he wins this war and comes here?" Job asked. "The Italian army is helping the Germans. They're in East Africa. I think I will go and fight this war."

Sipho was silent as he read the article. He thought about his father, and how worried he had been after a discussion with Mr Aaron about Hitler. Then he nodded decisively. "My father hated fighting. He said, 'War is terrible but Hitler is not a man you can talk to. You can't discuss things with such a man.' I know many men won't come back from this war, but we must fight Hitler."

*

When the army recruiting officers arrived, Job signed up immediately.

"Perhaps you should wait a bit, Sipho, until you're older . . ." he suggested again.

But Sipho was already signing his name beneath Job's, wondering where it would take them. Wondering what they would see.

Wondering if they would return.

*

And only later that night did Sipho remember Job's excited voice saying he had two bits of news.

"So, Job? What's the other news you had for me?"

"Good news: Zanele said yes!"

6

"We aren't idiots!"

Parkview, Johannesburg, South Africa
December 2014

As the car swung around a corner, the iPad slipped sideways off John's lap.

"Dad! I almost had a German fighter plane there," he grumbled.

"Why don't you look around you, John? We're in Joburg!"

"Look at what exactly? Houses and more houses!" But he closed his father's iPad cover and pushed his glasses higher up his nose.

It had been a five-hour drive from Durban. John stretched his long legs and flexed his back. His friends would be coming out of the surf now at Durban's North Beach. He pictured them with their surfboards tucked under their arms, dripping wet and too tired to talk. He'd been quite excited about his first trip to Joburg – they were spending two nights with a family friend in Parkview, and then a night with his grandmother in Soweto – but would it be worth missing four days of surfing?

"So, what's the plan when we're in Soweto, Dad?"

As Musi Matshoba drove alongside Zoo Lake, he seemed not to have heard his son's question. He was thinking of a holiday long ago, when he'd come here with the Punnett boys during their boarding-school years together in Swaziland. A black schoolboy in a whites-only suburb, breaking the law just by being there. They'd gone fly-fishing in Zoo Lake at five in the morning, before the police were about. The fish weren't even edible; they'd thrown them all back.

Musi chuckled softly to himself, and John looked at his father, puzzled.

What a weird time that was, Musi thought. And now he was back with his own children: fifteen-year-old John, and thirteen-year-old Zanele. Children born in a different time, and vastly different circumstances to his own. Children ensconced in excellent schools right here in South Africa, in KwaZulu-Natal. But it still astonished him that they had never even been to Soweto.

"So, what's there to do at Gogo's house?" John asked. "I bet we won't even get to see Soweto properly – Gogo's always too worried about wasting money. Mum says we mustn't spend the whole time on our cellphones, and I know Gogo's house is really small, so what exactly are we supposed to do? It'll be excruciating."

"Your grandmother will have something planned," his father said mildly. "It's only a –"

"We can play cricket!" John's sister, Zanele, interrupted. "Gogo can umpire."

"You think she's got a cricket bat?" John scoffed.

"Guys, you're only there for a day and a night. It'll be fine."

Zanele pulled a wry face and carried on writing in her wire-bound notebook, frowning slightly in concentration, her thick eyebrows almost meeting in a dark, straight line across her pretty oval face.

Her father glanced in the rear-view mirror. "What are you writing, Zanele?"

Another story the editor of Discovery Box *probably won't like*, she thought, and sighed. "A story."

"A true story? For that magazine you like?"

"They're *supposed* to be true, but I don't know any interesting true stories. So I invent them. My writing's OK – they're just not interested in fiction. The editor said I could try talking to my grandparents, but Gogo's life sounds so boring. Mum says she just worked all the time."

Musi shook his head in exasperation as he thought about his mother-in-law, MaGumede. She was such a stubborn, gutsy old lady. He had often asked her to move to Durban to live with them. She didn't want charity, she had told him. She liked to be independent. In Soweto she could live on her nurse's pension, with her friends all around her. In Durban she'd be lonely.

"Let me at least make your house more comfortable," he'd tried to persuade her.

"Save your money. Everyone spends, spends instead of saving!"

He had not insisted. His wife had a PhD and now taught at university because her widowed mother had saved to pay her fees. But twice a year he sent the old lady a plane ticket to Durban and now, for the first time, the children were coming to her.

He worried a bit about packing the two of them into her little house, though. And how would they get on with her neighbours? She was used to her grandchildren's outspoken manners, or their lack of manners, but he hoped they wouldn't offend the old lady's friends. Maybe it was best to broach it with them now, he thought.

"Guys, on Saturday, when you go to your grandmother . . . I'm sure you'll remember to be polite to everyone. She's from a different generation. She and her neighbours may not be used to children who speak their minds."

"*Dad!*" Zanele said crossly. "We aren't idiots!"

"Zanele, that's *exactly* the kind of thing I'm talking about!"

"*They* expect children to be seen and not heard," John laughed. "And you like us to question everything."

"I do!" His father spoke firmly. "But that is not the traditional way, not for Gogo's generation."

"It's OK, Dad. Chill! We'll do as you say, not as you do," Zanele told him, gazing out the window.

"Do you know the way to Jo's house, Dad?" John asked a few minutes later as Musi turned into a tree-lined avenue.

His father nodded. "We go back a long way, the Matshobas and the Punnetts. I remember her road runs from Zoo Lake to the golf course. The Punnett boys and I walked all over Parkview, usually very early in the morning, when I stayed here with them once, long ago. We'd walk under these huge old trees. Every street an avenue."

John and Zanele nodded and they looked out at the gracious old houses in slightly unkempt, leafy gardens. Jo Punnett often came to Durban; they'd known her all their lives. Their dad and one of Jo Punnett's sons were close friends, and now colleagues at the university, and the children were all friends.

"This is it – we're here!" Musi announced with a flourish as he stopped the car outside a wooden gate in a shaggy hedge.

John jumped out of the car and was ringing Jo Punnett's doorbell just as a WhatsApp message came through on his cellphone from Ted, Jo's grandson.

"*Remember crashed Messerschmitt at war museum.*" John read aloud. "Dad, Ted says the war museum's nearby. I must see the fighter planes! How 'bout we go tomorrow?"

"But what'll I do at a war museum?" Zanele demanded as Jo Punnett opened the gate.

7

Running out of time

Soweto, South Africa
December 2014

Up on the hill above Diepkloof, Soweto, a piet-my-vrou called, "Phezu komkhono!"

MaGumede paused as she reached towards a branch of her apricot tree. She lifted her head and listened for the call again. Instead she heard the low voice of her neighbour, old Mr Sipho Ndebele, talking to his daughter, Tabela. She usually loved the cheerful lilt of his old-style isiZulu. But today she heard a deep sadness in the words that wafted over the wall.

"Listen to that bird, Tabela! Phezu komkhono – it's time to hoe your land. My mother loved that bird call. Today I've been thinking about my friend Job, when we were prisoners of war . . . Such a thing he did on that ship, there in Tobruk. We told the colonel. We told him what Job had done. And the man who painted a picture of Job, he told the colonel too. But the colonel would not change his mind. So no one heard about it. And then after the war, that was such a tragedy . . . "

"Yebo, Baba," Tabela interrupted. "You are always talking

about that war these days. Why now? All my life you didn't mention it. Now you are ninety-one years old, and all you want to talk about is Tobruk, and those mountains."

"In Abyssinia. Ethiopia now," he murmured. "I was too busy before . . . And maybe I could not bear to think about it."

"Whatever, Baba! That war was over long ago, nearly seventy years ago. I'm sorry, I haven't got time to listen to your stories. I'm hurrying . . ."

MaGumede liked Mr Ndebele, a gentle old man of quiet wisdom. He'd recently been ill and could no longer drive the taxi he'd owned for many years.

"Not a mini-bus taxi. A silver Jaguar for weddings and important events," Tabela had made sure MaGumede knew. "My father loves driving his beautiful car." But after a heart attack he'd given his treasured Jaguar to his grandson Dumi, and had come to live with Tabela, who was a grandmother now herself.

MaGumede wondered about these war stories Mr Ndebele wanted to tell. What had he done in Abyssinia and Tobruk? And what was the tragedy? Such a pity his daughter wouldn't listen to him, she thought. Tabela was certainly busy, raising four small orphaned grandchildren and looking after her aged father, but MaGumede wished she would find time for him. His heart was failing. *He* was the one running out of time.

Next door the gate opened and Tabela stepped into the road. She was a large woman with a strong chin. She looked over the wall and saw MaGumede picking apricots.

"Making jam, Mama Gumede?" she called. "I should do that. My plums are ripe. But it's so dangerous boiling sugar in a crowded kitchen. Even the old man gets in my way."

"Morning, Sisi!" MaGumede greeted Tabela with a happy smile. "Not jam. I've got my grandchildren coming to visit from Durban, my Zanele and John. They're coming on Saturday. I'm cooking for them."

"Staying here?" Tabela put her hands on her comfortable hips and stared at her neighbour. "But your grandchildren are big!" She jerked her chin at MaGumede's house. "Where will they sleep?" She gave her own larger house a satisfied glance.

MaGumede prickled a little. "Oh, it's all sorted out," she said firmly.

Her daughter had only phoned the day before.

"Just an idea, Mama!" her daughter had said. "Musi's driving to Joburg tomorrow. He's got a meeting in Joburg and a conference nearby. The children want to go with him. They can spend a couple of nights in Parkview with Jo Punnett, and she can bring them to you Saturday morning. Back home Sunday afternoon. What do you think?"

"I'd love to have them!" MaGumede had replied, pushing aside any doubts in her happiness to finally have them stay with her.

Now she spoke calmly to Tabela. "They're coming to see me. I always visit them in Durban, or sometimes we go to Cape Town together. They've never been here."

"Yo!" Tabela was pessimistic. "Tricky! Children from a wealthy suburb."

"You can stop saying *yo*! Go now and do your shopping!" But MaGumede could never stay cross for long, and she smiled suddenly and added, "Sisi, you'll meet them on Saturday. Bring the old man, and your grandchildren."

Tabela shook her head. "The children are gone. Their uncle

Dumi came just now to take them for the weekend to give me a break. I'm too old to look after small children and a very old man who is sometimes like a child. When I'm busy in the kitchen he wants to be there too, always getting in the way, and he just stares at nothing. Or he wants to talk about things that happened long ago. That war in Abyssinia and Tobruk. I feel bad I don't have more time for him. Will you check on him while I'm out?"

MaGumede smiled sympathetically and nodded. Tabela started on her way, but then she stopped again and looked thoughtfully at MaGumede.

"Do your grandchildren know about the Second World War?"

"Strange question! John does. When he was little, if you asked him what he wanted to be when he grew up, he had only one reply: a pilot. So I got him a book about a fighter pilot, a South African called Sailor Malan. John loved that book. He lent it to his friend Ted, and even now the two of them collect books about war planes . . . Sisi, you met Ted's grandma, Jo Punnett. She came for lunch," MaGumede added.

Tabela nodded. "Untidy grey hair. A real magriza."

MaGumede gave a wry smile. "We both have grey hair."

"But not untidy." Tabela thoughtfully smoothed her carefully braided extensions.

"Now John has a computer game he loves, pretending to fly a World War II plane, a Spitfire. But that's all the flying John'll ever do – his eyesight's not good."

"So he likes stories about the war?" Tabela was silently making a plan: if the old man could come over and tell John and Zanele his stories, she'd have the kitchen to herself. She smiled broadly. "Good! I'll bring the old man on Saturday," she said decisively.

MaGumede nodded, wiped her hands on the apron covering her elegant, slim skirt, picked up her basket and strode back into her kitchen. Tabela admired MaGumede's tall, straight back.

"That old lady! She always looks good, even when she's cooking! She's so tight with money, almost never spends a *thing*, and then she gets a new outfit every year from the best dressmaker in Soweto. But what is she *thinking*? Her grandchildren, from a big house, coming to this tiny house!"

She shook her head as she bustled off again, her hair extensions and wide floral skirt swinging.

*

MaGumede's little house looked across a valley to where a great hospital stretched along the horizon. Her road was a cul-de-sac, with neat houses in tidy yards, most with a fruit tree or two. Some had wooden extensions, either joined on to the main house or standing nearby. High on the hill behind, half-hidden by tall trees, were the stylish houses of wealthy Sowetans.

MaGumede shut her kitchen door, plonked her basket onto the kitchen table, and sat down despondently. Tabela was right. How would suburban teenagers cope in this matchbox house? She looked around her, seeing for the first time how her grandchildren might see it. Just one bedroom and a kitchen. John's mattress would have to be tucked under the kitchen table.

"That will be a first for him." Through the window she looked at the wooden outhouse. "Oh dear, another first – the outside bathroom and toilet! An umkhukhu! Will they have even seen one before?"

From the shelf against the wall she picked up a thin, homemade booklet covered in stiff plastic, and gently ran her hand over the cover picture of a pop singer in front of an audience.

"*The Hip Hop Concert* by Zanele Matshoba," she read aloud to herself, picturing her granddaughter, who'd been attached to notebooks and pens from the moment she could write her own name.

That child loves to write stories, she thought with a wry smile. *Well, if she hasn't got anything else to do here, she can write a story about her gogo's little house and she can illustrate it with a picture of the outside bathroom!*

A flash of colour caught her eye. Against the far wall was a row of large plant pots, bright with red geraniums. She looked at the lemons on the tree by the window, and at her apricot tree, heavy with fruit. In the corner of the yard she saw the gum-pole pergola where a grapevine shaded a white wire-topped table and six chairs.

She straightened her shoulders. *It's not too bad,* she thought. *And they'll enjoy my cooking.* She tipped the apricots into a pot, squeezed a couple of dozen lemons and then stepped next door to see how Mr Ndebele was doing.

"It's so hot here, Mkhulu. Come and have a cup of tea under my grapevine where it's cool. I've been getting ready for my grandchildren."

8

"Why is everyone afraid of Rommel?"

A warm breeze was rustling the grape leaves overhead. Old Mr Ndebele finished his tea, placed the cup carefully on the table and sat back. The breeze here in Diepkloof was pleasant, not like the scorching, dusty wind in Tobruk, he thought.

The old man stared, unseeing, at the pots of red flowers, thinking of his first sight of Tobruk. He remembered standing with a group of South African soldiers at the rail of a small ship as it nudged into the harbour and dropped anchor in deep water just before sunrise.

*

Tobruk, Libya, North Africa
14 June 1942

With their kitbags over their shoulders, the men peered through the haze as they waited for the gangplank to be lowered on to the barge that would take them ashore.

"We fixed the Italians in Abyssinia. Now we'll fix them here!" a junior officer bragged to another.

"Not so fast! Rommel wasn't in Abyssinia, but he's here in the Western Desert, helping the Italian army," the other officer replied.

Who's this man, Rommel? Sipho Ndebele wondered.

He smiled to himself when the officer added, as if to answer his question, "That German general's the best in the world! And his army, the Afrika Korps. That's what we're up against."

"Better than our Danie?"

"Probably. And Uncle George."

Sipho was surprised. He didn't think there could be many generals more capable than General Dan Pienaar and General George Brink, who had led the South African troops through fierce and triumphant battles against the Italian army in Somaliland and Abyssinia.

Tobruk was a dismal sight. The rising sun shone orange against fallen stones and bricks. Not many buildings around the harbour were still intact; most had been damaged by bombs or shells. Sand blown down from the surrounding desert piled against the ruins. Further along the quayside the sand had almost covered hundreds of lorries lined up in rows. Sipho looked at them with interest.

They look South African, Sipho thought. *Why are they half-buried in sand?*

The heat already pressed down on his temples and flies swarmed around his head as the men continued to file off the ship and onto the barge.

"So this is what happened to Tobruk when the Aussies were trapped here." The first officer was speaking again. "How did they keep the Germans out?"

"Deep anti-tank ditches, around the perimeter of the town.

And concrete barriers, land mines and rolls of barbed wire. Our air force and the RAF helped. Our fighter planes chased the Luftwaffe bombers away, or shot them down, and we dropped boxes of food so the Aussies didn't starve," the other officer rattled on as the barge chugged to the dock.

On the quayside, two lorries were waiting. Sipho walked behind the officers towards the front lorry, but stopped when he thought he heard his name.

"Sipho! Woza! Sipho!"

The voice was familiar, but maybe he was just missing home.

"Sipho! Woza! Sipho! Come here!"

And there was Job, with an elbow resting on the open window of the second lorry, a wide grin on his face.

"Gibela! Climb aboard!"

The two officers and most of the soldiers drove off in the first lorry as others climbed on to the back of Job's lorry. Sipho got into the cab.

"Sawubona, Job! I didn't see you in Abyssinia. I looked for you." He noticed the insignia on Job's shoulder. "Nice stripe, *Lance Corporal Maseko!*"

Job laughed, and tried not to sound surprised as he said, "You too, *Lance Corporal Ndebele*. You must be the youngest lance corporal in the army . . . "

Sipho picked up the questioning tone: how could such a nervous, under-aged kid like him have been promoted? Sipho never spoke of his promotion in Abyssinia. He'd been surprised himself. And what was there to tell? *I was a driver* . . . There were thousands of men like him, he thought. "It looks as if there was a big battle here in Tobruk," he said instead.

Job nodded. "Yes. But the Aussies were here, not the South Africans. *Long* battle – eight months. They were trapped here by Rommel and his German army. Rommel couldn't get his tanks across the anti-tank ditch, so he hammered Tobruk with shells and bombs. The Aussies held out – they didn't let Rommel's army into Tobruk."

Job started the engine and followed the first lorry up the steep road from the harbour.

"The Aussies escaped the bombs for months by living in narrow slit trenches. Like desert rats," Job continued. "And then one day, Rommel got tired of being attacked by our air force. Pulled his Afrika Korps back and just went away. Maybe they were running out of food. Or petrol. Then the Allied ships came into the harbour and relieved the Aussies."

Job drove surprisingly fast over the bad road to the barracks, where everyone suddenly seemed to be in a hurry. Sipho tossed his kitbag onto a stretcher and was immediately issued with instructions to deliver petrol drums to the train station with Job.

"I could drive another lorry," Sipho suggested after the first load, as he and Job sped back to the petrol depot for more drums.

Job shook his head. "There aren't enough."

"But I saw plenty of lorries at the harbour," he said.

Job laughed ironically. "South African lorries! They came from Mombasa by ship. But the British engineers have decided they are 'no good for desert conditions'," he mimicked.

"I drove my lorry more than thirty thousand miles in East Africa," Sipho said. "Plenty of it through desert. To Nairobi, through Somaliland to Abyssinia. Back to Nairobi. Many, many times."

Job nodded, exasperated. "But our lorries sit here, even though there's all this petrol to move out. And we must hurry."

The lorry was climbing up the steep road onto the bleak plateau. All around, Sipho saw only jagged stones on rough ground that was dotted with low, sharp-leafed grey bushes. He was about to ask what the hurry was when Job pointed in the direction of a dip, about half a metre deep.

"That's an anti-tank ditch. When the Aussies were here the ditches were deep, with steep sides. Sand storms have filled them in, but we don't need them any more. We're leaving Tobruk in a couple of days. Auchinleck, the British general, doesn't want our army to get trapped here like the Aussies were," Job explained. Drums clunked against each other as they turned fast onto a wide, stony road. "Rommel's on his way back here with his Panzers. That's why we're moving all the petrol. Don't want to leave it for them," he added.

"Panzers?"

"German tanks. And not any old tanks. Panzers are fast! Deadly! Rommel's got hundreds of them, and 88mm guns that can fire two miles ahead."

Sipho listened in silence, marvelling at what Job knew.

"I often get to drive officers," Job continued as if reading his mind. "Sometimes generals, and I hear what they say. Last week I drove the other British General, Ritchie, with our General Klopper."

He swung the lorry onto a slip road towards the station, and then parked with a squeal of brakes next to a train. They jumped out to offload the petrol drums before the next lorry raced up behind them.

"Those two British generals keep contradicting each other. Ritchie told Klopper we should stay here and fight Rommel. But Klopper told him that General Auchinkeck said we must get a move on out of here. And we must get all this stuff, petrol and food, out of Tobruk. Then all the troops, fast as we can. If Rommel comes now, we won't be *trapped* by the Germans, we'll be *flattened* by their Panzers."

Two British soldiers ran up to help Job and Sipho. They laid planks from the back of the lorry to the train carriage, and rolled the drums onto the train before Sipho and Job swung back into the cab for the next haul.

"Andrew! Samuel!" Job called out in greeting to two men as another lorry drove up. "This is Sipho, he is umkhaya, my homeboy."

The driver of the other lorry, a muscular young man with bright, lively eyes, who Sipho understood to be Andrew, leant out to get a good look at Sipho.

"So, has he been organising you all your life?" he asked with a grin. "He organises all of us here. Sometimes even the officers."

Sipho laughed. "Yes! Thank goodness, or I don't know . . . "

The other man, Samuel, nodded at Sipho with a bit of a smile as Job reversed and sped away, back along the straight dirt road.

They were silent for a while in each other's company.

Sipho was wondering, again, about this man called Rommel.

"Everyone seems afraid of Rommel," he eventually offered.

At the petrol depot Job pulled up next to a ramp.

"That Rommel. Clever like a fox. It's sensible to be afraid of him. He's cleverer than our generals. General Auchinleck thinks we'll have a better chance against Rommel at El Alamein. So all this petrol's on its way there."

"Why El Alamein?" Sipho asked.

"Near El Alamein the way is narrow," Job grunted, as he wrestled yet another heavy petrol drum across the back of the lorry. "The sea is on one side and on the other side, just a few miles away, the sand is soft and swampy. Too swampy for tanks. It's called the Qattara Depression."

Sipho tipped a drum slightly, and swung it towards Job, who added, "Rommel's army will only be able to travel between the sea and the Qattara Depression. Our army and our tanks will be waiting for him. We must stop Rommel there, before he can get to the Suez Canal."

On the way back with the loaded lorry, Job stopped when he saw two British officers waving for a lift to the station. They squashed into the wide cab and spoke to each other as if Job and Sipho were not there.

"It's unbelievable!" one of the officers said in a plummy Oxford accent. "General Ritchie and General Auchinleck now sitting pretty, somewhere near El Alamein, maybe Cairo, leaving thirty-three thousand troops, and all our supplies, with a completely green South African general!"

"What does this Klopper know about fighting a war anyway? Until a few months ago he was sitting at a desk pushing a pen!" the other officer agreed. "He's been quite brave, apparently, but bravery isn't enough against Rommel. Strategy's the thing. Rommel plays chess on the battlefield."

"If it's chess we're playing, we're missing the queen. Nothing to protect us. Fighter planes, bombers, *the whole lot*, have left. We'd better get a move on – Tobruk's a death trap!" the first officer added.

"Like I said . . . " Job muttered in isiZulu to Sipho.

The next day they were up at dawn, shunting more petrol drums to the station. After several trips they parked at the petrol depot and climbed stiffly out of the lorry.

Job stretched his aching back and tapped the stripe on Sipho's shoulder. "Sipho, you haven't told me what you did in Abyssinia. A seventeen-year-old lance corporal?"

Sipho was about to say his promotion was a surprise to him too when a sergeant major raced up in an armoured car. He skidded to a stop nearby, followed by several empty lorries.

"Stop what you're doing! Leave the petrol! Everyone here! At the double! New instructions!"

Soldiers gathered as he spoke, staring in disbelief.

And Sipho never did answer Job's question.

9

"Dig for Your Lives!"

The sergeant major pointed towards the south-west perimeter of Tobruk.

"The tractors are there already, and spades and shovels. The lorries will take you. Dig out that anti-tank ditch – that's where Rommel will attack. Get busy!"

No one moved.

What's he saying? Sipho thought. *We'll be far away from Tobruk when Rommel arrives . . .*

"At the double!" the red-faced sergeant major shouted. "Lance Corporal, these officers need a lift. Take them in your lorry. NOW!"

The officers sat in front with Job. Sipho and the others climbed hastily onto the back and Job drove them to the south-west perimeter of Tobruk. At the dip that had once been an anti-tank ditch, the soldiers picked up spades and started digging while Job returned to the barracks to fetch more men.

Within the hour, almost three thousand men, British and South African, white and black, were digging there, side by side. With sand in their faces, their eyes, their ears; sand dug out of the trench slipping back in, the men shovelling it up again. They used tractors to try push the sand away, but still the ditch was not deep enough to keep out a Panzer.

And still they didn't know why they were digging instead of getting away from Tobruk.

When Job returned for the final time, he picked up a spade and joined Sipho and Andrew, who were working together.

"The officers were talking..." The men listened while they dug. "Orders from Churchill, Prime Minister of England: Auchinleck has told Klopper we can't leave Tobruk!"

"Does Churchill know there are no anti-tank ditches?" Andrew asked despairingly. "That we've got no planes? Does he know *anything* about Tobruk?"

Job shook his head. "If we must stay here and face Rommel, my friends, we'd better dig for our lives!"

*

For hours they dug, muttering that the generals and Churchill must all be mad.

"Why this side of Tobruk?" Sipho asked Job in between heaves of the shovel. "Why are we digging, here, in the south-west?"

"The Germans are coming from the west. But there are huge rocks in the west and the north-west, so the generals probably think Rommel will attack here," Job panted. "No one knows how close Rommel and the Afrika Korps are, and there's no reconnaissance plane to find out," he added, peering up suddenly.

Sipho and Andrew followed his eyes, and there tiny against the sky, was a plane with the black-and-white crosses of the German Luftwaffe under its wings.

"A Messerschmitt," Job murmured.

"Rommel will know pretty soon what we're doing," Sipho said, and Job grunted as he sank his spade into the slippery sand.

A platoon of soldiers was sent across the half-dug ditch. They walked into the desert, placing landmines in the sand to blow up German tanks.

And still the others dug. They dug all day and all night and the next day. And when at last the ditch was ready and no tanks could come into Tobruk on the south-west side they thought, *Tonight we will sleep.*

But there would be no sleep that night.

10

"What's that clanking?"

As the sun went down they heard a deep, distant rumbling, growing louder.

"Bombers!" someone yelled.

They looked up at the darkening sky and there they were, coming over the horizon. Hundreds of bombers. A minute later the planes were roaring above them. Bombs screamed in the air. Phweee! They hit the ground. Doff!

"Duck!" Job yelled as he and Andrew rolled into the ditch and pulled Sipho in after them. The ground shook and it did not stop shaking.

All night the bombs dropped, the sound moving eastwards. Sipho lay huddled in the ditch. He tried covering his ears to keep out the sound of bombs but felt the thumps reverberate through his bones.

By the early light of morning they could see the bombers flying over them; the sky was dark with planes. Now German Stukka Dive Bombers swooped low dropping bombs. Messerschmitt fighter planes raked the ground with gunfire. Most had the Luftwaffe's black-and-white cross; some had the white stripe of the Italian air force.

Sipho and Andrew and Job stayed hunched down.

"So many planes!" Sipho said. "Swarms of them. Like bees. Locusts. And not one of ours!"

"Ours are too far away," Job reminded him.

The bombing moved further east. They heard the crump of bombs falling in the distance, but even with shell-fire from the Germans' big 88mm guns coming closer, it was time to get out of the ditch.

They ducked as they ran.

"Lance Corporal Maseko, I need you here. We need drivers. Round up any drivers you can find!" the sergeant major called through the chaos.

"Here's another driver!" Job pointed at Sipho.

"You drive?" The sergeant major looked at the skinny teenager, but had no time for doubt. "Our gunners need food and water, Lance Corporal! Get those pots of soup to our gunners over there." He pointed to a panel van. "Maseko! We need drivers *and* transport! Hospital's bombed, and I don't see any ambulances. Dressing station's down there. Get the wounded men out of here."

As Job ran off, Sipho dashed to the driver's side of the van. Bullets clattered into the door. He felt the thumps of both the bullets and his heart; his mouth was dry.

He drove in zigzags and parked behind a ruined building next to the platoon of gunners, handing out army biscuits and mugs of soup, filling water bottles. A gunner fired, but Sipho could see it was no good against the Germans' far-reaching 88s.

How long will these gunners survive? he wondered as he dashed amongst the soldiers with soup and water, nearly deafened by bombs but still hearing the screaming of both shells and the wounded.

In the hours that followed, he saw men maimed, wounded. He saw men die.

In the evening Job came by, collecting wounded men, using a door as a stretcher. Sipho helped Job lift a man whose right leg was missing below the knee. They placed him on the door and laid him in the back of the lorry with others, wetting his lips with a water bottle. Job tore his shirt into strips for bandages.

They had become used to the sound of distant bombs on Tobruk's eastern perimeter, but then Sipho thought he heard another sound.

"Listen, Job!" he said. "What's that clanking?"

"The Panzers are here," Job said, and he tied a tourniquet around the man's thigh.

As they helped wounded men onto the lorry, Sipho watched for the tanks to appear, to attack them where they were, on the south-west side of Tobruk. The sound grew louder.

And then fainter.

"They've gone . . . " Sipho whispered to himself, not quite believing it.

Some men thought the tanks must be going straight to El Alamein, and they were relieved, almost jubilant. Not Job.

"Rommel is clever like a fox! He's not going away," he insisted. "He's planning something. This is not the time to be happy!" he added firmly, before driving off to find the dressing station with his load of wounded men.

A few minutes later an armoured car drove up, and Sipho watched General Klopper climb out and hurriedly inspect the anti-tank ditch. Most of the soldiers who had been digging were still there and there was a rush towards the General.

"The tanks have gone away, Sir! We heard the tanks go past!" a British corporal called out.

"But the German troops are coming. What must we do with no guns?" a black private asked.

General Klopper looked at his troops, amongst whom were more than a thousand black soldiers, none with guns.

He said something to a captain alongside, who ran to the general's car and spoke briefly on a radio. When he came back, he was clenching his fists.

"Sir! That *fool* of a quartermaster won't unlock the ammunition strong-room. He won't give out arms and ammunition without a direct order from headquarters, *in Cairo!*"

"Tell the quartermaster I have fourteen hundred Native Military Corps men milling around here with no arms!" General Klopper said.

The captain spoke again on the radio, and then he and the general drove off to attend to other urgent matters on the far side of Tobruk.

The black soldiers did not get guns from the quartermaster.

Late in the afternoon they saw two planes with the red, white and blue circles of the RAF flying high above them.

"Our planes at last! Kittyhawks!" Sipho said.

"Only two," added Job in disgust.

The Kittyhawks dropped a few bombs far away, and flew off again.

Throughout the night bombs continued to drop on the south-eastern perimeter of Tobruk. Some of the men found a place behind a broken wall, hoping to sleep now that the tanks were gone, and while the bombing was in the distance.

But Job shook his head. "Hhayi khona, that fox-man has another plan."

Just before midnight Sipho lay down and shut his eyes. For two days and a night he had dug. Bombs had dropped all of the next night, and all of the next day. Now he dreamt the wind was rattling . . .

"Panzers!"

He was yanked from his exhaustion just as it felt his eyes had closed.

In the silvery dawn light Sipho saw a Panzer tank silhouetted on the hill, pointing its long gun straight at them and within moments Panzers were streaming down the hills all around them, like hundreds of ants. Great billows of smoke swirled up from the town and the harbour. And there from the east, on the hill behind the tanks, came thousands of German soldiers.

"They're everywhere," he murmured.

"What a mess!" Job was saying. "Rommel sneaked back in the night. He's bombed the concrete barriers on the south east and brought the Panzers straight in. They've come past the Indian and Scottish regiments, down to the harbour and now up here. We have no guns, and there are landmines behind us. We can't retreat. We're trapped!"

11

"Every man for himself!"

Columns of German soldiers moved briskly down the hill with more Panzer tanks crawling behind them. Italian soldiers trailed behind the tanks. The Germans opened fire. As bullets flew past them, Sipho and Job hunched, frozen for a few seconds, and then scrambled for cover. Allied soldiers returned fire but could not stop the mass of German soldiers as the tanks rolled closer.

A lieutenant ran by, shouting to a captain, "Phones have been bombed! General Klopper can't give instructions. What should we do?"

"Lance Corporal Maseko!" the captain called to Job. "Get a message to the General. Most of the South African 2nd Division are trapped here!" He held out a note and Job darted off.

Just minutes later two British officers drove by holding a small white flag and shouting through a loud hailer, "Every man for himself! Escape if you can! We are surrendering! General Klopper's instructions: *Every man for himself!*"

A wind blew off the desert. Thick dust eddied around the armoured car.

Few German soldiers saw that little white flag and the shooting did not stop.

Shell fire screeched and thumped, machine guns rattled. Sipho could not see Andrew. Job was gone. Should he try to escape through the landmines? What would Job do? Two doctors and three hospital orderlies ran from the bombed hospital towards the anti-tank ditch.

"There are landmines out there!" Sipho called to them.

As they scrambled across the ditch and started running over the minefield, Sipho heard two explosions. Five men, two explosions: those were the odds.

A shell thumped close by, and he dropped flat on the sand. He needed to get somewhere safe, and started running the other way, dodging low between wrecked vehicles and through bombed buildings, towards the army headquarters.

An officer called calmly through the chaos, "Where's Lance Corporal Maseko? I need someone who can get things done! Or Private Mahudi! Where's Andrew Mahudi? Or Private Smith! Johnson? Is there *no one* reliable here?"

Sipho stepped forward. "I'm here, sir! Ndebele."

The officer looked at Sipho: just a kid, but a lance corporal, he noticed. And the German troops were closing in. "Ndebele! The Germans haven't seen that idiotic little flag! We need a big white flag." He pointed to the half-bombed army headquarters. "Tie it to the roof! We're surrendering!" He jumped into an armoured car and sped off through the gunfire.

Sipho stared after him and then looked at the headquarters' building. He'd be visible for miles around. A target.

He didn't move until another rattle of gunfire shocked him into action.

Where would he find a big white flag?

Nearby were the ruins of the hospital. There were sheets in the hospital. Sipho bent low and ran between the ruins. He shoved the hospital's broken door aside and looked into a ward. There, amongst the remains of beds, he found a dirty white sheet. He tied it to a broomstick.

Bending low, he sprinted to the headquarters, climbing up the rubble and out onto the shattered roof. A strong gust blew off the desert, buffeting him as he straightened up. He staggered and sat down hard astride the roof ridge. Bullets clattered against the roof tiles next to him. He tried to drive the broomstick in between the tiles, but could not get purchase. He would have to stand again.

He planted his feet on the tiles and was half standing, rocking in the wind, when he felt hands on his ribcage, stretching him upright.

"Kahle! Steady!" Andrew's voice.

Sipho rammed the broomstick between two cracked tiles and it held fast. As he and Andrew slithered and scrambled to the ground, the wind lifted the dirty white sheet and Sipho heard it, flap, flap, flap.

The guns went silent.

Flap. Flap.

*

Old Mr Ndebele stirred. He sat up and gave himself a shake. He was sitting under the grapevine; MaGumede's washing flapping in the warm breeze.

"Oh! You're awake, Mkhulu! I thought you were sleeping. Another cup of tea?" MaGumede had come out with her laundry basket and began to pull her dry sheets off the line.

"No thank you, Sisi. No more tea. I was not quite asleep. Just remembering . . . " he started, but she smiled at him and picked up the laundry basket. Pushing the kitchen door open with her hip, she went inside.

He remembered the silence. It had lasted a long moment.

And he remembered seeing German soldiers everywhere he looked. They were not shooting. They seemed surprised. Stunned. They pointed their guns at the South Africans. The silence suddenly ended and they screamed in German, "For you the war is over! Drop your weapons! Hands in the air!"

Andrew laughed sardonically at the German soldiers and asked, "What weapons?"

They understood his mocking tone, but not the words, and they crowded in on him and butted him in the ribs. He clasped his chest and bent over, and the South Africans and other Allied soldiers understood then that they were prisoners of war.

When they'd joined the army they'd known they might be wounded, even killed. They had not thought they would surrender, and they were ashamed.

The next two days were the worst, old Mr Ndebele thought to himself. *We were marched into the desert on the road to Gazala and we thought we would die there, left in the sand, with the flies and nothing else.*

Except a dog, he remembered suddenly. *What a thing to remember.*

12

"Do you know why you're fighting this war?"

Heat rippled up from the desert sand and a brilliant light woke Sipho. Awake all night, he had shivered until the sun rose and warmed his chilled body, and only then drifted off to sleep. Now a white-hot sun baked the sand. Sipho lifted his aching head from the khaki hat he had used as a pillow. His eyes were gummed shut and gritty. He licked a finger, gently wiped away the sand and squinted ahead.

A skinny, mangy dog seemed to be floating towards him above the heat haze.

A dog inside the barbed wire? Floating?

Am I going crazy?

He opened the other eye and saw all four paws padding on the ground as the dog snuffled through the loose sand.

"If you're looking for something to eat, don't bother. No hope of that," he told the dog bitterly. "No one here has eaten for two days. We've been dumped in the desert to die."

The dog looked at him.

Nearby, a group of officers sat together murmuring quietly.

"No hope now. Rommel's on his way to El Alamein. He'll probably wipe out the rest of our army," he heard one say.

"We'll be saying 'Heil Hitler!' in a couple of months," agreed another.

Off to one side their commanding officer sat alone, his elbows on his knees and his head down, the sun burning his white neck scarlet. He had been there all yesterday, all night and now today, hardly moving.

The dog sidled up to him and raised a leg against his humped back. A dark stain appeared on his uniform. The dog turned and lifted the other leg. The commanding officer did not stir, and the dog ambled away into the haze.

That was how we all felt, old Mr Ndebele remembered. *Hopeless and ashamed, dying of thirst and hunger.*

He shuddered as he remembered the chaos two days before, when the German soldiers had suddenly confronted thousands of Allied soldiers. At first the Germans hadn't known what to do with their prisoners of war, so they'd screamed at them and shot into the air, and then herded them together, just as they were. Some prisoners had water in their water bottles; most bottles were empty. And many men had not eaten since the day before.

The day had dragged on. Their officers were lined up and marched away. Italian soldiers arrived and stood pointing rifles at the tens of thousands of Allied men. A German officer had shouted into a loudspeaker and the German soldiers had left to fight, leaving the Italians guarding the prisoners.

The captured men were marched away from the town, away from the sea and into the desert. The sun beat down and the temperature soared.

"A death march," someone muttered.

Hours later, several men had collapsed and were helped by their friends.

When a big, open German car drove by, a whisper went up the line: "There's our General," and Sipho had seen a German officer sitting stern and silent next to General Klopper.

"Rommel," went another whisper.

Sipho stared hard at the man who had made even Job afraid.

Far out in the desert the prisoners of war were told to stop. Lorries drove up with rolls of barbed wire. The Italian guards ordered a group of prisoners to unroll the barbed wire around the massed men, making an enormous cage: twenty-four thousand men, and sand. Nothing else but the Italian guards pointing their guns at them.

No water, no food, no blankets and no spades to dig toilets.

Late that day the Allied officers joined the men in the enclosure. Each officer had a greatcoat, a blanket and a water bottle. But for two days the other prisoners, white and black, had nothing. Men were thirsty and scared.

Fights broke out. The British soldiers bitterly mocked the South Africans.

"Thirty-six hours before your general surrendered. What are you South Africans made of?"

Sipho did not often get angry, but he walked up to the British soldiers and said with quiet menace, "If your quartermaster had given us guns, we would have fought."

Job pulled him back into a group of men. "Choose your battles, Sipho!" he muttered. "Save your energy."

The next day the Scottish and Indian troops, the last to

surrender, were marched into the camp. The number of prisoners of war had swelled to nearly thirty-three thousand. They still had no food and no water. All day they sat on the desert sand with their backs to the wind. Flies settled around their eyes and noses and mouths.

And in the night they thought they would die of cold.

"Like an oven in the daytime and cold at night as Joburg in winter," Job said.

On the third day lorries brought drums of water and boxes of dry biscuits, and spades to dig toilets. Each prisoner was given two biscuits and half a cup of water a day. They felt human again and organised the camp.

A week later they were each given a piece of corrugated cardboard to sleep on.

That night Sipho bit into a corner of the cardboard so that his teeth would not chatter, and he slept a little. The next day they were each given a greatcoat and a blanket, and a few days later tents arrived, and more food, but still not much: they were always hungry, always thirsty.

One morning Sipho heard a strange rumble, "rommelrommelrommel".

The same big open car drove into the camp and the prisoners moved like a wave towards the car. The sound got louder: "Rommel! Rommel!"

The fox-man was visiting them in the barbed-wire camp.

Sipho was standing on a slight rise and had a good view of Rommel's car. A British captain and a lieutenant stood nearby. As the prisoners of war surged around Rommel the captain said worriedly, "We have a problem. This is an *enemy* general and our troops think he is some kind of demi-god. And he's talking to them. Chatting. What general *chats* to troops, especially enemy troops?"

"Field marshal," the lieutenant corrected him despondently.

"What?

"*Field Marshal* Rommel. Guards say he's been promoted. His reward for hammering us."

Sipho saw Job in the crowd and hurried down to him. Together, they moved close enough to hear Rommel speak.

An officer asked Rommel why they were given so little water. Rommel laughed and said, "You are getting the same as me. We are all short of water. I also get half a cup a day."

Then a white South African sergeant asked why he must live with black soldiers.

Rommel looked surprised. He glanced at where some prisoners were queuing for food: whites and blacks in different lines.

"Prisoners of war are to stand in the same queue, black and white together," he said firmly, and then gave a bitter laugh. "I wonder if you men know why you are fighting this war."

Sipho was confused. *A German field marshal teaching white South Africans how to behave decently? Rommel must know Hitler wants a pure white race. Does Rommel know why he's fighting Hitler's war?*

Rommel was now giving instructions to the Italian guards: "Treat all these prisoners of war well. They are brave soldiers, same as you."

As Rommel climbed into his large car Sipho heard him add, "Brave men, like lions, but their generals are donkeys."

*

For the rest of their years in the Western Desert, black and white soldiers in the South African army queued together because Rommel had told them to do so. Sipho often heard soldiers say Rommel wasn't so bad, seemed quite a good guy, made sure his POWs were not badly treated.

How can they think that? Sipho wondered. *Thousands of our men have died because Rommel's fighting this war for Hitler.*

*

Many decades later, as he was flicking between channels on the television, Mr Ndebele came across an interview with the German director of a new movie about Rommel. Even the sound of Rommel's name brought a sheen of sweat to his brow. He turned up the volume.

"Rommel realised he'd made a terrible mistake supporting Hitler. He plotted to get rid of him. But the plotters were betrayed and the Gestapo made Rommel drink poison." The interviewer sounded almost regretful.

The director responded firmly, in a strong German accent: *"Rommel may have been chivalrous, but his victories simply prepared the way for the Nazi extermination machine."*

Sipho thought of Mr Aaron's cousins who had disappeared, been *exterminated*. He slapped his hand on the arm of the chair.

Yes! That's why I feel no regret.

*

Once Rommel and the German soldiers had left the camp, the Italian guards didn't bother to treat them well any more. An aeroplane with a big red cross dropped boxes next to the camp and the guards let the boxes lie outside the barbed wire until a German officer visited and told the guards to let the prisoners of war have the Red Cross parcels. There was food in the boxes, writing pads, envelopes and stamps, and playing cards.

Early one morning, lorries drove into the camp and the Italian guards called for all the black prisoners to line up. Job and Sipho climbed onto a lorry and they were driven down to Tobruk harbour.

When they returned one of the South African officers came to speak to them.

"Where did the guards take you?" he asked. "What did they make you do?"

"We had to load petrol drums and ammunition onto a ship," Job replied.

The officer went to see the most senior Italian guard to discuss the Geneva Convention, which Germany and Italy had signed.

"You are not allowed to make POWs do war work," he insisted.

The Italian sneered at the officer. "They aren't soldiers. Show us their guns! Soldiers have guns!" He shrugged and walked away.

The next day the white prisoners of war were taken in ships to Italy, and later trucked to camps in Germany and Poland to join thousands more Allied prisoners of war. Many were never seen again. Some died on the long marches they were forced to take across Europe, others in snowy prison camps, where thirty-three thousand died in one freezing winter.

And in Tobruk, the Italian guards made the black prisoners of war work in the harbour, unloading and reloading the ships. The Italian guards were more brutal now that the Allied officers were gone: many used their sticks, some used their guns. One day a prisoner was slow to obey a shouted order and muttered angrily under his breath. An Italian guard pulled out his gun and shot him.

Sipho saw the shooting. He was sick with terror.

Fear and depression made most of the prisoners sluggish and slow, but not Job.

"Hhayi bo! We aren't going to sit and do nothing just because we're POWs. We must keep fighting Hitler!"

And he did, old Mr Ndebele thought to himself.

A minute later his daughter came bustling through the gate. She called her thanks to MaGumede and helped her father home for lunch, and for a while he forgot about Tobruk and Job and the ship.

13

The painting at the top of the stairs

Saxonwold, Johannesburg
December 2014

"Ditsong: South African Museum of Military History," John read the sign as Musi drove through a pair of wide wooden gates on the hill above the Zoo.

"I don't know what *I'm* expected to do here for two whole hours," Zanele grumbled.

"Make the best of it!" Musi replied. "My meeting's important. I'll be back at five to pick you two up."

In the car park John and Zanele waved goodbye to their father before making their way to the impressive archway that formed the war memorial. Above the arch a tall green angel gazed out over the zoo and across the vast forest-like stretch of trees dotted with rooftops. And beyond, the Magaliesberg range, a blue smudge on the horizon.

"Phew, it's beautiful here. Doesn't look like the middle of a city," Zanele murmured.

"More trees in Joburg than in any other city in the world," John confirmed. "The planes I'm wanting to see are inside the hangars. A Spitfire. And the first jet fighter plane. Ted says there used to be a Messerschmitt with its nose stuck in the ground so it looked like it'd crashed here, but they moved it inside. Let's go find them."

Zanele rolled her eyes, but followed her brother.

From the foyer they saw three small aeroplanes lined up in a glass-fronted hangar on their left.

"*The Sailor Malan Hall,*" John read. "He was one of the greatest fighter pilots in the war."

He stepped inside the hangar and stood with his back to the high glass wall. Each plane had a black-and-white cross on the side of the fuselage and under the wings. The first plane had no tail fin and no wheels. Its belly was flat on the floor and the propeller blades were twisted and bent. On the tail fin of each of the other two planes was a swastika, the Nazi symbol. John's lips parted and his eyes widened as he looked along the row of planes.

He pointed at the first plane. "This is the crashed Messerschmitt, an ME 109, hit by a Spitfire pilot during the Battle of Britain. These were the best fighter planes – they could climb really high and attack with the sun behind them. But then came the Spitfires. This Messerschmitt pilot probably didn't even see what hit him."

Zanele sighed, but she peered over the rope barrier at the wrecked plane and its curled propeller blades.

"Sort of like flower petals," she murmured.

John took a deep breath. "This is amazing – a whole bunch of Luftwaffe fighter planes. That far one is the first jet fighter. Unbelievably fast. Lucky the Germans didn't make them till the end of the war. If they'd made them earlier, they'd have won for sure." John was mesmerised by the jet fighter's menace.

"Looks like a shark!" Zanele shuddered.

John pointed at the strange bits of wire on its nose. "It was a *night* jet fighter. That aerial's for radar, to find its target in the dark," he added.

"So did they fight here, in South Africa?" Zanele asked.

"No! These planes were brought here after the war. The South Africans fought up north, in East Africa, and in the Western Desert – Lybia and Egypt. Later, Italy."

"I'm not interested in your boring fighter planes . . . " Zanele said, and wandered off up some wide stairs. She read the captions of the photographs lining the walls. At the top of the stairs she stopped in front of an oil painting of a man with a chiselled nose and high cheekbones.

A painting of a black man, she thought to herself. *Not many of those in this museum. I wonder what he did.*

She stood on tiptoe to read the brass plaque.

"Job Maseko MM," she read aloud. "What's MM?"

"Military Medal," she heard from behind her as a woman with a pleasant smile came and stood next to her. "It means he did something courageous and was awarded a medal."

"Oh! When?"

"World War II," the woman replied.

Zanele shook her head confidently. "My brother knows a lot about World War II, and he's never mentioned black South Africans in the war."

"Actually, more than forty per cent of South Africa's forces were African, coloured or Indian. A hundred and forty-three

Job Maseko MM

thousand. In the army, air force and navy. Stretcher bearers and ambulance drivers in the thick of the fighting. And lorry drivers with dangerous cargoes, often under fire from enemy planes, driving across wild terrain with no roads. All providing supporting services."

Zanele had hardly taken her eyes off the painting, but now she turned her wide eyes towards the woman, who, she noticed, was wearing the name badge of a Ditsong museum worker.

"But when you say 'supporting services', do you mean they weren't involved in the fighting? Surely everyone in the war was?"

"Well, no. Black men in the war weren't given guns. Not at first, except for coloured soldiers in the Cape Corps. And never officially, except in Madagascar. Guns from captured Italians were sometimes given to black drivers so they could defend themselves. And we know from black veterans of El Alamein that they were given .303 Lee Enfield rifles, and were trained to use them before the battle. But there's no mention of that in the records."

"And this guy? Did he have a gun?"

"Job Maseko had no gun."

How weird, Zanele thought. *Sending men off to war without any guns.*

The woman pointed at the painting. "You had to do something exceptionally brave to win a Military Medal. In fact, Job Maseko was recommended for the Victoria Cross, the highest accolade. Major Sinclair and Colonel Sayer nominated him, but Colonel Smith didn't want a black person to get the VC, so he was given the Military Medal instead. The war artist Neville Lewis heard about it, and asked to paint Job's portrait. He usually painted famous generals – Smuts, Montgomery and men who won the VC or the DCM."

"Did other South Africans in the war win the Victoria Cross?" Zanele prompted.

"In World War II? Yes. Four South Africans won the Victoria Cross. Many more won the Military Medal though," she replied, "and quite a few of them were black men."

The woman pointed down the stairs to a glass case. Inside was a dilapidated black box with knobs and a speaker. "Job Maseko got hold of that radio when he was a prisoner of war. He heard what was happening at El Alamein and he was able to plan his –"

A phone rang in a nearby office.

"I've got to get that. There's the library – you'll find more information there," she told Zanele, pointing towards a door before hurrying off.

Zanele wandered through the swing door into the small museum library, where a young librarian was tidying books on a shelf.

"I'm looking for info about that guy in the painting, Job Maseko," Zanele said hesitatingly.

"Give me a minute." The librarian dashed off and returned with a book and a yellowing page mounted on cardboard from *The Star* newspaper, as well as an old copy of *Drum Magazine.* "Here. You'll find some information in these," he told her. "Job Maseko was a prisoner of war, captured when Rommel's army overran Tobruk."

She picked up the book – *The Unknown Force: Black, Indian and Coloured Soldiers Through Two World Wars* by Ian Gleeson. She scanned the pages until her eye caught the name "Job Maseko".

Here's my true story!

She took out her notebook and pen.

*

Zanele was not aware of time passing until the librarian startled her.

"We're closing in five minutes," he said. "I need to put these things away."

"OK!" she replied. "I'll Google more when I get home to Durban. Thanks!"

She closed her notebook and ran lightly down the stairs, two at a time, to look for John. She found him in another hangar looking at a little silver plane.

"Where've you been, Zanele? Hope you've kept yourself out of trouble. This Spitfire's a beauty, hey," John said without waiting for her reply.

Zanele found that she was quite interested in the plane now that she was learning a bit more about the people involved. She looked at the plane carefully, imagining what it would be like to be inside it.

"It's tiny! The way you've talked about them, John, I thought it'd be more impressive."

"It's a one-seater. The Spitfire pilot was also the gunner, so it could be small. It's got a Rolls Royce Merlin engine, though, so powerful the pilots sometimes greyed out as the plane took off. Sailor Malan trained Spitfire pilots in England. Spitfires like this won the Battle of Britain," John claimed grandly.

"I like its wings. Nice shape."

"Elliptical."

"Hmm, I still think it looks like a toy. So, John, *I've* found something *really* interesting! A painting of a black South African who won a medal in the Second World War. Come see it quickly, before the museum closes!"

"In World War II? A *black* South African?" John didn't move.

Zanele nodded. "There's a painting of this guy, Job Maseko. Come see! He was a prisoner of war at Tobruk. Have you read about him?"

John shook his head and then turned and followed her into the main building. "Half the books I read are war stories, and I didn't know there were any black South Africans in —"

"When he was a prisoner of war, Job Maseko used that radio to listen to the news so that he knew what was happening and could make plans . . . " Zanele interrupted, pointing at the radio in its glass case as they hurried past it. She was enjoying her new-found knowledge — at last she knew more than her know-it-all brother. "And here he is!" she said as they reached the painting. "Job Maseko MM! That means 'Military Medal'. And there were twenty-nine!" she told him.

"Twenty-nine *what*?"

She sighed. "Twenty-nine black South Africans won the Military Medal. And, John, that's a pretty big deal, because black South African soldiers weren't even armed!"

John turned back to the painting. "His eyes look like an eagle's . . . as if he's scanning the horizon."

Zanele waved her notebook at him. "I've been looking for a true story, and this is it!" she said excitedly.

"You said an old person had to tell you a story."

"Well, I wish I could hear Job Maseko tell his story, but he died long ago so he can't tell me. But this is the story I want to write!" she said firmly.

Behind them, the librarian locked the library door and then walked past them on the stairs. Zanele smiled her thanks at him.

"I think we'd better go, or we'll get locked in." John whipped out his phone, took a photo of the painting and they hurried out of the museum

"And *do you know*, Job Maseko had a fiancée with my name! She was also Zanele! I read all about it . . . "

They stood waiting in the car park for a while with Zanele chattering away about her namesake being in love with a brave soldier.

"So?" John said at last, a bit irritated. "Are you going to tell me? What did he do?"

"Oh! Job Maseko sank a ship!"

14

True grit

Their father's car pulled up next to them.

"Sorry I'm late. Jump in!"

"Hi Dad," they muttered, but barely paused before carrying on their conversation.

"Oh yeah, Zanele, I'm gonna believe you! Blew up a ship? What with – a torpedo? You said he didn't even have a gun!"

"You think you know everything, John."

"Well, if it's about World War II, I know plenty!"

"It says he had twenty bullets." Zanele handed John her notebook with the handwritten copy of the citation.

"OK . . . " John said after a few moments, "so he had a fuse. Must have been a long one," he said dubiously. "You can't blow up a ship when you're still on it!"

Zanele waited as John read on.

"And anyway, it doesn't make sense! Even if the ship blew up after the POWs got off it, the military police would have guessed it was them who blew it up! And those guys had some pretty gruesome ways of making people talk. Someone would have spilled the beans and the military police wouldn't have bothered with a trial. Job Maseko would have been shot for sabotage . . . Zanele, are you sure you got it down right?" John jabbed his finger at Zanele's writing.

"It's all there!" Zanele snorted.

"Well, except for an explanation for why they weren't caught!" John shook his head, and then looked, unseeing, in the direction of the distant Magaliesberg mountains. "Job Maseko sinks a German ship in Tobruk harbour and doesn't get caught," he mused. "Why not? He must have delayed the explosion. I wonder how we could find out how . . . The war ended seventy years ago. There can't be anyone alive who could tell us."

"I didn't know there were black men in the South African army," Musi chipped in from the driver's seat.

"There were loads, Dad," Zanele told him, perking up again. "More than forty per cent of the army. I'm gonna write about this, Dad! *This* is my true story!"

*

John jumped out of the car as soon as it stopped at Jo's house.

"Jo! I need to skype Ted from your computer!" he called. "I mean, *please* may I?" he mumbled as he raced down the passage.

"Sure!" Jo's head popped around the kitchen door. "It's all set up in my study. Give Ted my love . . . " she said to John's retreating back.

In the study, John pressed the button to open the computer, and waited impatiently for it to start. Soon Ted's face appeared on the screen.

"Hi Ted. Just got back from the war museum. Have you ever heard of black soldiers in World War II? South Africans, I mean? I've never read of any . . . ?"

Ted took a while to answer. "Not sure . . . I've never really thought about it. But hang on! My great-grandpa, Jo's dad, was a captain in the war. There's a photo of him with a black driver . . . And I think he saved my great-grandpa's life . . . Something about a hyena. Ask my grandma – she'll remember. Why d'you ask?"

"Zanele discovered something at the war museum about a black soldier . . . "

"John!" Zanele appeared in the doorway. "That's *my* story!" She walked across and looked over John's shoulder. "You'll be able to read about it in *Discovery Box*, Ted. Anyway, John, you have to come help carry stuff outside for supper."

"John, before you go, ask my grandma if we can borrow that old trout rod of hers. I have my two little brothers here wanting to go fishing with us next week, and we're short of a rod."

"OK. Oh, and your grandma sends love. Bye!" John closed the computer.

"I don't think you should get too excited about this story of yours, Zanele," John said as he helped his sister carry platters of roasted vegetables onto the verandah.

"Why?"

"It'll be like starting a jigsaw puzzle when you know there's a piece missing. How will you ever finish the story when all the guys *must* be dead?"

*

Outside, Jo had her carving knife poised above a juicy roast chicken as John and Zanele came through the old teak doors on to the verandah, which overlooked a wide lawn and a wild profusion of flowering shrubs and climbing roses.

"Your house is so comfortable, Jo," Zanele said, pulling one of Jo's basket chairs up to the table and sinking into a pile of cushions.

Jo laughed. "You mean not smart? Certainly not elegant, like your mother's lovely house." She looked at John, her deep-blue eyes quizzical.

"Why the hurry to Skype, John?" she asked.

John pulled out a chair and sat down at the table. "I wanted to ask Ted if he knew about black soldiers in the South African army in World War II. He told me about your dad. He said a black soldier saved your dad's life in the war. From a hyena."

"I haven't thought of that for a long time." Jo expertly carved a chicken leg. "My dad was asleep in his tent. The driver shouted to wake him, and he woke to see the hyena's teeth above him. It was about to bite off his face. Can you *imagine*! The driver fought off the hyena with a stick because he didn't have a gun. My dad told us he didn't know what surprised him more: the hyena or the young driver's bravery. I remember him saying, 'He was very young, and very frightened, and very brave! When it mattered, he came up to scratch. That's *true grit*!'"

She waved the carving knife to emphasise the words, and John ducked comically out of range.

"High praise from my dad. He didn't dish out compliments, and his language seems so old-fashioned these days. There was something about a lion too . . . I can't quite remember." She wrinkled her forehead. "The driver's quick thinking also saved them from an Italian convoy, but I've forgotten the details. Oh, we loved hearing those stories! My dad tried to find the driver after the war. Wrote to the mine, but . . . " She shrugged. "There's a photo of the two of them somewhere, with their catch of trout. Chicken, Musi?"

Musi held out his plate. "*Trout?*" he asked in surprise.

"They were in the Abyssinian mountains. Army food was tinned bully beef and what they called dog biscuits. My dad said it got a bit boring and fresh fish made a change, so he took along his rod," Jo replied. "You know my family and trout fishing!"

"I do! This is where I learnt to fly fish. In the mucky Zoo Lake."

"But not for trout!" Jo laughed. "Can you believe that was twenty-five years ago!"

"Oh, Jo," John suddenly remembered the message. "Ted asked if he could borrow your old rod." Not wanting to be sidetracked, he added, "And he told me about the photo from World War II. Can we see it?"

She nodded. "Sure. In fact, that's the rod that went to Abyssinia. Ted can have it. I'll get it, and the photo, after supper. Oh, and the cricket gear you asked for. Pass your plates please, Zanele and John."

Zanele silently passed her plate. She was deep in thought. She would start the story with Job wanting to get married and needing money for lobola, the bride price.

"Did your dad tell you anything else about the war?" John asked Jo.

"My dad hated war. He only joined up because of Hitler and the Nazis. So he told us about his adventures, but not really about *war* . . . Here you go, John. Tuck in, everyone. I remember something about their big army lorry getting marooned, with the sump stuck on a rock, when they were crossing a shallow river. It was raining and the river began to rise. They looked for a flat stone to put under the jack but all the stones in the river were round. The jack kept slipping, so they battled for hours into the night, until the river had risen up to their waists. They were so tired that, at two in the morning, they decided to go to sleep in the back of the lorry and if they got washed away too bad."

"And?" John asked.

"The next morning the sun was shining, the lorry was still upright, the flood had shifted it and they drove out."

John swallowed and laughed. "Lucky! Jo, I love roast potatoes. These are brilliant."

She passed him the bowl. "Help yourself to more then. The only really scary thing my dad ever told us was that he and the driver were given army-issue suicide pills in case they were caught by the Askaris – those were the Abyssinians who supported Mussolini and his fascists."

"Suicide pills? Why?"

"Because Askaris were known to torture people they thought were spies."

"And was he?" John asked.

"Was he what?"

"A spy!"

"No! He was a scout. In army uniform. They were driving their lorry overland, looking for a second route through the Abyssinian mountains in case the Italians blocked the Marda Pass," she explained.

John quickly helped himself to another few roast potatoes. "And? Did they find another route?" he asked with his mouth full.

"I don't know, but they didn't need it in the end. The Italians tried to block the Marda Pass, but our army and air force pushed them back, so we didn't need the second route after all."

The conversation between Musi and Jo drifted to other topics, while the teenagers ate silently, each contemplating what they'd just heard.

"Now, you two," Jo snapped them out of their reverie, "if you will take your plates to the kitchen, I'll get the photo. I've sometimes wished my dad's driver had that photo. A memento of his time in the war. And John, dear, please bring the bowl of cherries. That's the nearest I got to making pudding."

A minute later they all returned to the table, Jo with a battered black photograph album and a DVD.

"Thought this might interest you: *The Battle of Britain*." She handed the DVD to John. "The hero is based on our Sailor Malan, the fighter pilot. For some reason they call him Skipper in the movie." She pulled a wry face. "You can watch it after supper if you like. My dad had such hopes for Sailor Malan's Springbok Legion after the war. He thought the Springbok Legion and the Torch Brigade might be able to resist the apartheid laws, but . . . Everything they fought for was destroyed."

"This is great, Jo, thanks! I've got the computer game of *The Battle of Britain*. I was playing it on the way here."

"Good. Enjoy." Jo reached for a cherry and slowly turned the pages of the photograph album until she came to a page with several small black-and-white photos: one of a long lorry travelling overland, one of a mountain stream, and an indistinct photo of an officer holding up a string of fish while a black soldier held a fishing net. At the top of the page was written, "Fluff in Abyssinia."

They all leaned over to look.

"Your dad's name was *Fluff*?" John asked.

"Nickname. Hardly anyone knew his real name . . . " She pointed to the man holding the net. "And this is the man who saved his life."

15
Military police

In Diepkloof, Tabela's house was quiet. She sighed with pleasure as she switched on the television to watch a programme she'd saved.

Enough football! At last the old man is asleep, she thought to herself.

But old Mr Ndebele was not asleep; he was lying back comfortably in his bed remembering.

They were five friends: Job, Andrew, Samuel, a man from Cape Town called Koos, and himself. Most of the prisoners of war had sat all day with drooping shoulders, staring into space. But not Job's friends. The old man remembered how Job's energy had lifted them all. In his mind old Mr Ndebele could see Job standing in the centre of a group, hear Job's voice telling them that even POWs could help win the war . . .

"We can't stop fighting just because we're locked up! What will happen to us if Hitler wins? Keep your eyes open. Look for things we can do. If you're near an Italian lorry, one teaspoon of sugar in the petrol tank will mess up the engine."

Sipho had done that. Put a little sugar from his Red Cross box into his pocket and, when the guards weren't looking, he'd dropped it into the Italian lorries' petrol tanks. One lorry here, one there. He'd heard a German officer complaining about those "no-good Italian lorries".

He chuckled quietly at the memory.

And he remembered Job pretending to lose his balance when they were loading machines onto a ship, exclaiming in pretend dismay when a big machine fell overboard. He remembered Job rooting around in the desert sands of the prisoner of war camp, kicking at objects and bending down to pick up others. He had joined him.

"What are we looking for?" he'd said as he bent down to help.

"I don't know," Job replied. "When I see it, I'll know."

Sipho had found an empty condensed milk tin. So he had a cup. Job had found bits of wire, fuse wire, like they'd used in the mine. He'd joined them together to make one long wire. Sipho had watched him measure it. What was he planning? Then Sipho had found a cigarette packet with one cigarette, and later a box of matches. He'd wanted to smoke the cigarette, but Job had said, "No! It'll be useful."

Job had also found bullets, twenty unused little bullets, the gunpowder still inside them. He asked for Sipho's tin cup and he hid all those things in the sand under his cardboard bed. He didn't say what he was planning, and Sipho didn't ask.

The next day all five friends had been working together, loading drums of petrol onto a barge, when they saw a German supply ship arrive in the harbour. Another barge had taken the prisoners of war to where the ship was anchored in deep water.

A big, burly old Italian guard showed them where to put the petrol.

"We'll *hammer* those Greeks," the old Italian guard had

boasted, while Job and Sipho worked in the hold, untying nets and rolling out drums.

Against the far side of the hold they saw boxes of ammunition.

"Petrol and ammunition in the same hold? This guard's not too bright!" Job said. "Tomorrow Franco will be back to guard us." He seemed thoughtful.

The next day they were told to load several hundred more drums of petrol destined for the German army in Greece, and Franco was their guard . . .

Even now, seventy-three years later, old Mr Ndebele's stomach knotted as he remembered what had happened on the ship's deck that day. Andrew had jostled Franco around, brazenly using his elbows to get the young Italian guard to face out to sea while they danced. And Mr Ndebele remembered Job jauntily reappearing just before they had filed down the gangplank to be taken back to camp.

He remembered waiting for an explosion, but thinking that too much time had passed. *The fuse wire wasn't long enough to burn all that time*, he'd thought to himself. *It must have fizzled out.*

At the camp they'd sat outside their tents, as usual, making the most of the cooler evening air. Sipho had been wondering if it was relief he felt, or disappointment . . .

KaBOOM! Doff! Doff! Doff!

Sipho had looked at the darkening sky, checking for planes, for bombers. No planes.

It was Job's doing.

*

They did not ask him. They did not want to know.

They *must* not know.

There was no view of the sea nor of the harbour from the camp but down between the hills, red and black plumes rose like fire in the sky, like a sunset in the wrong place. That night they went to bed very late, the sky still red.

Just before dawn the next morning, Sipho looked out at the dark sky, worrying.

Would the guards realise? But it seemed to be orders as normal, and the unknowing guards took them to the harbour for another day's hard work.

Except that the ship was gone.

Drums and wooden planks floated in the oily water on the far side of the harbour. The camp guards were puzzled, thinking at first that the ship had sailed off in the night. But it was only half loaded; there on the quayside were rows of petrol drums ready to load.

Then someone told the guards about the fire.

The prisoners of war stood around waiting, pretending they didn't know what the fuss was about.

"We were pretty good actors," Mr Ndebele murmured to himself.

A motorbike with a sidecar came roaring down to the harbour. Two members of the German military police jumped off and spoke angrily to the Italian guards.

The military police were coldly methodical as they examined the harbour and the debris.

The prisoners of war continued to act unconcerned as the military policemen questioned them with quiet menace, asking if they'd seen anything different on the ship, or a big red mine floating in the harbour. The prisoners of war pretended to be a bit stupid. "Angazi," they all replied; they knew nothing.

And Sipho prayed that the military police wouldn't connect South African gold mines, with their dynamite and fuses, with South African prisoners of war.

*

After the two military policemen drove off, the prisoners weren't sent to work in the harbour again. Perhaps the military police guessed they had something to do with the explosion, but how could they have caused an explosion so long after they had left the ship, and from so far away?

They were taken instead to a workshop, where Job soon progressed from sorting and stacking equipment to fixing broken radios.

That's how he knew what was happening at El Alamein . . . Old Mr Ndebele stretched and yawned, smiling as his eyes closed.

16
"The news today from El Alamein..."

The military policemen had left Tobruk, but the prisoners of war were jumpy and tense.

Franco, the young Italian guard, was manning the gate one evening when they returned to camp, and Sipho saw him glance at Job with an odd look, not quite a smile. What did the guard know? Had he guessed? Would he say something? Was Job safe?

Sipho had also noticed that Job had been unusually subdued for a few days. And then, one day, Job was suddenly cheerful again, singing as he sorted through the spare radio parts.

That evening, as they sat in the cool breeze, Job told Sipho and Andrew that they wouldn't be locked up in the POW camp much longer.

"Rommel's on the run. We're beating the Germans at El Alamein! The rest of our army, with the 1st South African Division, will be here soon to free us," he told them.

"How do you know that?" Sipho asked, amazed.

"BBC News. I fixed a broken radio that was chucked out. Our Danie's been in the news for quite a while. He's been holding out against Rommel at El Alamein. And now there's a new general there: Montgomery. General Montgomery, and our Dan Pienaar, are pushing Rommel back."

"So our 1st Division is doing alright there at El Alamein?" Sipho felt a flush of relief. "I wonder what General Pienaar would have done if he'd been at Tobruk instead of Klopper?"

"D'you mean would he have obeyed orders, like Klopper, and kept us in Tobruk, sitting ducks for Rommel? Maybe not. Who knows?"

"I'd like to listen to the news!" Sipho said.

"If the guards catch us with a radio they'll shoot us!" Job warned.

Sipho knew that, but he wanted to hear this news. He thought of his father, and how interested he would have been. After dark, he slipped out with Job, Andrew and Samuel. They hunched low and ran through the shadows to the almost flattened remains of a bombed hut. Job lifted the floorboards and there, wrapped in a sack, were a radio and a big battery. He connected the battery to the radio and turned the sound low. The men huddled close.

At first they heard crackles and then dongs, like Sister Katherine's school clock, and then a man was speaking. He speaks just like a British officer, Sipho thought.

"This is the BBC. Here is the news. Today Rommel's troops were pushed further back from El Alamein . . . "

The radio crackled again and the voice became inaudible. Job turned the dials but for a few minutes they heard only static. When he found the station again the news was over and they heard a different voice speaking between the crackles, letting the whole world know how Rommel had been defeated at El Alamein.

"*The only possible approach to El Alamein from Tobruk is between the sea and the Qattara Depression. The German army had to use that route. General Montgomery, who replaced . . . crackle, crackle . . . was waiting. Montgomery out-foxed the Desert Fox at El Alamein.*

"*He hid our tanks, the new tanks from America, in a steep valley on one side of the approach. And then . . . crackle . . . built tanks out of cardboard, phony tanks, on the other side, so Rommel prepared to fight from the wrong position.*

"*The Prime Minister said in a speech today to the House of Commons, 'Now, this is not the end. It is not even the beginning of the end. But it is, perhaps, the end of the beginning.'*"

When the bulletin finished, Job grinned and unplugged the battery. "So, with clever generals and new tanks we've got Rommel on the run. Maybe we can win this war. Until now I wasn't so sure."

He buried the radio again beneath the floorboards and they returned quietly to their tents.

The next morning Job's tent was empty, Samuel's too.

The guards were distracted with other matters, and none seemed to notice that Job and Samuel weren't there. But Sipho was worried: Job must have escaped into the desert. He wished Job had told him, but he could hear Job's refrain: "The less you know, the safer you'll be." *What will happen to him if he's caught? How will he survive in the desert if he isn't?*

Andrew laughed off his concerns. "They'll be fine. When was Job not fine?"

*

Two weeks later they heard the boom of big guns in the distance.

The Italian guards scrambled to pack up their tents. They took all the food and drove away in the only vehicles, leaving the prisoners of war stranded in their desert camp, a very long march from Tobruk. The prisoners of war decided to stay there. A few hours later they saw a dust cloud and then armoured cars. They did their best to smarten up, wanting the relief party to see they had kept up army standards throughout their ordeal.

"What if they think we're Italians? If they don't know we're Allied POWs, they might start shooting!" someone called out.

Sipho made a second white flag

For the second time, Sipho hurriedly made a white flag. He found a towel the Italians had left behind and tied it to a tent pole. Waving the flag, Sipho walked out onto the road with a few others, all in tidy uniforms, but gaunt from months on iron rations. The British and South African armoured cars raced up and stopped next to the group of relieved soldiers.

"A welcoming committee!" an officer said cheerfully.

The barbed wire was pushed back. Lorries drove in with water and food, just enough for each man to have a small meal, but better than the dry biscuits they'd lived off for months. It was greeted with shouts of "Hip! Hip! Hooray!" three times by the prisoners of war.

Like the abelungu, Sipho thought, laughing. *What a ridiculous thing to shout*. But how wonderful it was to be free and to feel the regard and concern of the Allied soldiers after the careless neglect and cruelty of their guards.

They were ferried in lorries back to their old barracks in Tobruk where, that evening, a ship brought plenty of food. Boxes were opened and tins tossed to the lines of hungry men. Sipho caught a tin of bully-beef. Who would have thought he'd look forward to opening a tin of bully-beef? He happily licked grease off his fingers and munched an apple as he looked around for Job and Samuel. Surely they'd returned with the triumphant troops? But Job wasn't in the barracks. No one had seen him, or Samuel.

Thousands of people were milling about that night, so when Andrew again said, "This is Job you're talking about. He's a survivor!" Sipho decided not to worry: he hoped he'd see them in the morning.

But he didn't see them the next morning, or the next.

Day after day he looked out for them. Were they lost in the desert? Had they died of thirst? Had they been recaptured? He wondered bleakly if he'd ever know.

17

AmaDurbs meet amaJozi

Soweto, South Africa, December 2014

John and Zanele tossed their bags, the old trout rod and the cricket gear into Jo Punnett's car, and soon she was driving around the skyscrapers of downtown Joburg and then on the motorway, southbound for Soweto, past gum trees and veld.

"I thought Soweto was *in* Joburg, but it's miles away," Zanele observed after a while.

"Yes, but we're nearly there now. Look for a very long building up on your left, the hospital. That's where we turn off into Diepkloof."

A few seconds later Zanele called out, "There's the hospital!"

"That's Barra – Chris Hani Baragwanath Hospital – where your gran worked when she was nursing. We turn down here . . . and round this corner . . . and it's the house with red geraniums." Jo stopped the car.

MaGumede came out to open her gate. "Welcome! Bring the car inside, Jo!" she called. "Hello, bantabami! Hello, my children!"

John jumped out and helped his grandmother with the gate.

"Gorgeous geraniums, as usual, Beatrice!" Jo said as she edged the car inside and parked in the shade of the lemon tree.

John stood awkwardly looking at the house, trying to picture his mother growing up here. Where had she studied to get all those distinctions at school and university? He'd expected to see a small house, but their garage in Durban was twice this size!

Zanele wrapped her arms around her grandmother and squeezed her tight.

"And how's my special girl?" MaGumede asked.

"It's crazy we haven't been here before, Gogo!" Zanele said, swinging around to look. "I like your grapevine! It's a green cave there, under the pergola."

John hoped his grandmother hadn't seen his dismay. He leant over and pecked her cheek. "Hi, Gogo!"

Zanele was right, he realised. The pergola was lovely. In fact, the small garden was so pretty, so carefully laid out, it made the house look inviting. Maybe this was why his mother often spoke of simplicity and elegance: she had Gogo's sense of style.

"If you're thirsty, there's fresh lemonade. Don't worry with your things. We can sort them out later," MaGumede said.

But the children lugged their bags into the house, dumped them in the bedroom and then joined the two grandmothers, who were already sitting in the deep shade. MaGumede was dressed, as usual, in an elegant skirt. She wore a tailored blouse, with pin-tucked pleats, and a matching headscarf. Jo Punnett's idea of smart was newish jeans and clean trainers, but she had brushed her wild grey hair.

Zanele looked at the plump apricots sitting in a bowl on the blue-checked tablecloth.

"Help yourself, Zanele," her grandmother suggested. "But don't eat too many or you'll get a runny tummy." She poured the lemonade into glasses and handed one to Jo Punnett.

"Yes, Zanele. And if you get a runny tummy in the middle of the night, I'm *not* going to walk you out to the umkhukhu, even if you are afraid of the dark," warned John, grinning at his grandmother. *I bet she had a total panic about that umkhukhu,* he thought.

Zanele took no notice. "We brought some cricket things, Gogo. John's going to teach me to bowl a googly! You can umpire," she announced, wiping apricot juice off her chin with the back of her hand.

"A googly, Zanele?" John passed Jo a plate of shortbread squares, each with an almond stuck in it. "In your dreams!"

"Ah, I know these of old," Jo said with relish, taking a biscuit. Then she turned her head to listen. From the trees on the hill came the lovely falling call of a Burchell's coucal. "The rain bird!" she murmured.

"Yes. uFukwe, we call it. But I hope the rain will hold off today and tomorrow," MaGumede said anxiously, looking up at the sky, still clear and blue, but with meringue clouds piling high on the western horizon. They'd all be fine in her house, she'd decided, as long as the weather held.

*

By the time Jo drove out of the gate, the cricket bag had been unpacked and the stumps were set up in the road, which ended just a hundred metres further down the hill. Jo steered around the stumps, waved and drove off.

MaGumede brought a garden chair out to the gate. "There probably won't be another car here today, but keep an eye out. I want to see you bat, Zanele." She watched John bowl to her granddaughter, who wacked the ball up the hill. Two boys from further down the road had climbed on to their gate and were watching silently.

"If you guys want to play, you have to field before you can bat!" John called to them and they jumped down into the road.

"Heita, mehlo mane! Hi, four-eyes! I'm wicketkeeper!" one of them said decisively. He stood behind the stumps with his hands on his knees.

"Liphi ikasi?" the second boy asked in Soweto slang.

John and Zanele looked blank.

"Uphumaphi? Where're you from?" he explained formally, and just a little patronisingly, glancing at his brother.

"Siphum' eThekwini," John replied carefully. He tossed the ball to him. "And you're bowling."

"So it's you guys from Durbs against us?" the wicketkeeper queried.

"Yebo! AmaDurbs against amaJozi," John replied.

MaGumede sat back in her chair. Why had she worried?

18

Omagriza and an umadala

"Our grandmother's famous chicken curry, spicy potatoes and her own apricot chutney!" Zanele announced to John a couple of hours later, when they stopped their cricket match for lunch under the grapevine.

Clouds billowed above the grapevine and the shade had deepened.

Between mouthfuls John had been telling MaGumede about the war museum and the planes he'd seen the day before. "Thanks, Gogo!" he said, licking his sticky fingers. Then he looked out beyond the vines. "It's getting quite dark," he remarked.

A minute later a distant rumble of thunder echoed over the hill, and MaGumede gave a little sigh. What would John and Zanele do inside her kitchen all afternoon? All she had were a pack of cards and some old jigsaw puzzles.

John stood up. "We've probably got an hour before it rains. Let's beat the amaJozi, Zanele," he said, and they ran back out into the empty road.

The neighbouring boys swung over their gate and the cricket match resumed. In less than an hour, thunder cracked nearby and fat raindrops splattered on the steamy road.

"That's it, guys! Maybe we can play again when the rain's stopped," John suggested.

"See you later," the two boys called, and they dashed home through the raindrops just as a very old man with a walking stick stepped out of the gate next door. Behind him a woman in a bright floral dress held an umbrella above his snow-white head. The children waited under the eaves as the two slowly approached.

"Oh, great," John bent his head towards Zanele, whispering beneath the sound of drumming rain. "Now we have to spend the afternoon sitting inside being polite to two old, grey-haired omagriza and an umadala. This sucks."

"Don't be so rude!" Zanele whispered, digging her elbow into his ribs. "Gogo can't help it if it rains! Anyway, remember to be polite!"

Tabela came inside the gate and greeted them. "Sanibonani, bantabami. Hello, my children. I'm your gogo's neighbour. This is my father."

"Sawubona, Mama Tabela. Gogo said you and your father were coming to tea. Sanibonani, Mkhulu," Zanele said, smiling graciously. "Please come in." To John she quickly turned her head and pulled a face. "That's how it's done!" she whispered.

John grinned and helped the old man into the house, running back to bring in a garden chair, and they crammed around the table in the little kitchen as rain rattled on the metal roof.

"Sawubona, Baba. Sawubona, Sisi," MaGumede greeted. "Nasi isihlalo. Hlala phansi, Baba. Hlala, Sisi. Here's a chair. Sit. Sit." She helped the old man to a chair, where he sat, looking a bit vague, as she introduced her grandchildren.

"John, and this is Zanele."

Tabela looked first at the children, and then out at the rain. "Yo, Sisi, but your grandchildren are big. And now it's raining so they can't play outside," she said, looking oddly pleased as she sat with her hands in her lap.

The rain was falling straight down and it seemed to have set in – there was no wind to blow the storm over.

MaGumede nodded glumly at Tabela. This must be so boring for the children, on their only day with her, she fretted. She poured the tea from her pretty, old-fashioned teapot. And all the while the old man sat very straight, with his hands on his stick. He didn't seem to register who the children were.

Tabela was speaking again, "So, John, your gogo tells me you like to play a computer game with aeroplanes from the Second World War. You know about that war?"

The old man lifted his head and looked at John.

John nodded. "The computer game is called the Battle of Britain. You fly planes on the computer . . . flight simulation. You can fly a Spitfire or a Messerschmitt . . . " he petered out. *Do they have any idea what I'm talking about?*

"My father was there in that war, John. You should ask him about it," Tabela said, hoping she'd be able to slip off home in a minute or two.

The old man nodded at John. Then he turned to look at Zanele, and something like recognition suddenly flashed in his eyes. When he finally spoke, his voice was so quiet and frail that they all had to strain to hear him over the sound of the rain.

"I . . . think about it now, most days. For many years . . . I had no time, you see, when my children were growing and I was working two jobs. I was . . . a driver at the bank in the day.

Driving my taxi at night." He paused and seemed to choke on his words, slowly raising a phlegmy handkerchief to his lips. "All those years I didn't think about the war. Now I think about those places, and my friend –"

"I've got time to listen for a little while," Tabela interrupted gracelessly, "but I must go soon."

19

What did you do in the war, Mkhulu?

Mr Ndebele stirred his tea. He didn't look up, and he didn't see John lean forward, his face suddenly alert.
"The Second World War, Mr Ndebele? You volunteered? Why? And were you in East Africa or the Western Desert?" John asked.

The old man took a sip of tea and placed his cup back in the saucer before he answered.

"I was in both those places. First in East Africa . . . Kenya . . . and in Abyssinia . . . Later in the Western Desert . . . Tobruk."

"What did you do there, Mkhulu?" John pressed on.

Mr Ndebele was silent for a minute, remembering. "First we drove lorries. Hundreds of us. Thousands of miles we drove, over deserts, through swamps. Getting stuck in the sand, stuck in the mud."

"Where were you going? What was in the lorries, Mkhulu?"

"We took petrol, in big drums, and food and ammunition from Kenya to Abyssinia. And sometimes we took the men, the troops."

"So why did you join up, Mkhulu?" asked John, a bit surprised to find he was so interested.

Zanele ran to her grandmother's bedroom and was back moments later with her notebook and a pen. "Was it scary in the war, Mkhulu?" Zanele slipped in her question, hoping to get some interesting snippets for her story. "Were you often in danger?"

Imperceptibly, the two older women also leant forward to hear.

"It was dangerous, and I was afraid every day and every night for two years. But there was one good time, even though it was dangerous also," he answered in his low voice. He seemed to drift off into his own thoughts. "That was the time they gave me a different job. I had to drive a captain, there in the mountains, in Abyssinia."

"I want to know why black men joined up, Mkhulu," John insisted, interrupting.

For the first time, the old man looked up, directly at John, and his voice seemed louder and clearer than before. "We joined the army because we knew about that man Hitler, and his Nazis in Germany. The Nazis did not like black people and Jews. Bad things were happening to the Jews in Germany, and also to the black people there. If the Nazis came here, maybe the same would happen to us. So when men from the army came, there at the mine, and said we should fight against Hitler, and stop him from coming to South Africa, my friend signed the papers, and I signed also."

Mr Ndebele gasped and gave a strange, spluttering snort. They stared at him, startled, but then realised he was laughing. They waited while he wiped his eyes.

"That was when I learnt to drive! But those days – eish! – there weren't enough lorries to teach so many men. They were doing everything in a hurry, building the lorries, thousands of lorries, there near Port Elizabeth. And teaching thousands of us to drive. Yo! So they were teaching us with a wooden wheel on the end of a stick. That stick was stuck in the ground and we were sitting on a stool holding that wooden wheel . . ." The old man had to stop speaking because he was breathless with laughter.

The children smiled. He took a breath, cleared his throat and spoke again.

There weren't enough lorries

"The clutch and the brake were flat pieces of wood, also stuck in the ground. So we learnt like that, before we sat in a lorry. And when the new lorries came, we went in the train to that place, Broken Hill. Northern Rhodesia. Zambia now. And that was when we really learnt to drive. Hundreds, thousands of us driving the troops, there on the Great North Road. Three thousand kilometres of muddy, rocky track. We drove to

And then back again, and again

Kenya, through Somaliland to Abyssinia, and back. And then back again, and again."

"That actually sounds quite fun," said Zanele. "I thought you said you were scared every day for two years, but that doesn't sound too bad at all."

"My dear little Zanele, we were carrying petrol. When we saw the Italian planes, we worried about the petrol on the back of our lorries because maybe a bomb or bullets from fighter planes would hit the petrol. We were trained to stop the lorry and run and lie flat till the plane was gone. Because if you were hit like that . . . you could not survive. Now! Even now! When I hear a plane, I look up. I must check. Does it have our red, white and blue circle, or the Italian white stripe, or the Luftwaffe's black-and-white cross? It was dangerous, and I was afraid every day, but I loved to drive . . . "

"So were most of the black soldiers drivers?" John asked.

"Plenty were drivers, driving lorries and ambulances. But in a war you must be able to do more than one thing. In places like that, drivers must be able to fix lorries and ambulances, fix planes for the air force. Ambulance drivers and stretcher-bearers must also be paramedics. Other drivers worked with engineers to build roads and bridges, because often there were no roads."

He chuckled again.

"At first I was not such a good driver! I had not been trained in a lorry. And I didn't know how to drive with heavy loads on the muddy, rocky mountain passes. Yo! You could slide over the edge and fall down a thousand metres. But I learnt fast in those dangerous places. I knew I must get petrol, ammunition and food to the troops. Armies must have food. In the rainy season we drove through swamps and we got stuck, sometimes six, seven, eight times in one day. We must dig around the wheels and cut bushes to put under the wheels. Some places five days to drive ten kilometres."

Old Mr Ndebele's eyes drifted to the steamy window as he told them about the time he'd driven up a steep, steep pass.

It had been raining for days. It was still raining, and the road was like a river, just mud coming like a river down the mountain. His lorry danced in the mud and the wheels spun, and then the lorry slid backwards and sideways to the edge. And he could see, way down next to the river, another lorry, upside down, the wheels sticking up in the air. So he carefully turned the steering wheel a little at a time, and the lorry continued its slide backwards, all the way down. But it stayed on the road.

The officer came to his window. "Try again, Ndebele. We must get this food to the troops."

So he had tried again. This time he put his foot down, and drove fast. And when the lorry started to dance he steered first the same way it was dancing, even near to the edge. Then it obeyed him, and he could steer it away from the edge.

"When I was at the top, the officer came and took me down the pass on the back of his motorbike, and I brought all the lorries up that pass. He said I was a good driver. I was surprised! Many drivers were clever. I had only three years at school and I was quite young – I think I was seventeen. And always I was afraid. But I knew! This is what I can do. This is what I am. I am a driver. The sergeant major said I must teach the other drivers, the white drivers and the black drivers, how to drive up muddy mountains. So first they made me a lance corporal.

"One day a captain came to us. He told our sergeant major he needed the best driver for special work, and the sergeant major called to me, 'Lance Corporal Ndebele!'

"The captain was not happy. 'Looks a bit young,' he said.

"'He'll do sir,' the sergeant major said.

"So I did that special work in Abyssinia, driving a lorry into the mountains, without roads, without even tracks."

"Doing what, Mkhulu?" John asked.

"The captain said we must find another route through the mountains."

John sat back in his chair. That's also what Jo's dad had done in Abyssinia. Perhaps there'd been several scouts doing that work, he decided, and listened closely.

"It was beautiful there, but dangerous also. That lion! One time I was washing my clothes in the river and I looked up and a lion was watching me. Just three metres away. A big yellow lion, with a big brown mane, his eyes fixed on me. I had no gun, so I thought I should run, but my legs could not work. I heard the captain speak quietly: 'Don't move, Lance Corporal.'

"I stayed very still. The lion just walked away and the captain uncocked his gun. It wasn't hungry."

John and Zanele grinned at the old man, who added, "But I was more afraid of the Askaris than a lion. The Askaris helped the Italian soldiers. If they caught Allied soldiers like us, they tortured them. So before we went into the mountains the captain showed me the pocket in his rucksack, where there was a little silver box with suicide pills." He laughed. "But, as you can see, we did not need those pills."

20

A POW says he sank a ship! Not possible!

John did not laugh. He let out a slow breath. "I'm glad you didn't have to take those suicide pills, Mkhulu. It would be a sad end for such heroes. We know someone else who was given suicide pills in Abyssinia. Jo Punnett's father."

"I've met Jo Punnett." Mr Ndebele looked at MaGumede, who nodded. "So her father was there, in Abyssinia." Then he lent forward, eagerly. "But if we are talking about heroes, then I must tell you about my friend who won a medal. He was umkhaya, my homeboy. He always knew what was going on. He saw everything. His eyes were like the eyes of ukhozi . . . "

"An eagle," MaGumede translated for her grandchildren, whose isiZulu was not as good as she would have liked.

The old man nodded. "Like the black eagle. He was the one who said we should join the army because Hitler must be beaten. He had a fiancée, a beautiful girl, with your name," he said to Zanele. "And pretty eyes, like yours too."

She looked down, embarrassed. Then a thought struck her and she paged back in her notebook to the first sentence of her story: *Job Maseko needed to buy five cows to pay lobola, the bride price, to his fiancée's father. She was a beautiful young woman called Zanele.*

Zanlele opened her mouth to speak but John put a hand on her arm.

"Wait! Don't interrupt!" John said quietly as the old man continued his story.

"My friend joined up for two reasons: to get money for lobola, and to fight for freedom."

Zanele turned to John. "It's him! It's got to be him!" she whispered insistently. "He's talking about the same guy!"

"Shh!" John whispered back. "If Job isn't alive to tell his story, this is next best thing. So *do not* interrupt!"

"After Abyssinia I went to a terrible place. Tobruk. June 1942. We surrendered to Rommel's army and were POWs. Many, many thousands of us. And the general was South African so we were ashamed . . ."

"But, Mkhulu, General Klopper *had* to surrender to save your lives," John interjected, immediately forgetting his instruction to his sister. "I've read about this. Tobruk was the *only* major battle in the Western Desert where the Allied forces had no air cover . . . not a single fighter plane to keep the bombers away. And Rommel had *hundreds* of planes and *hundreds* of Panzer tanks. You would have been wiped out if you hadn't surrendered. There was nothing else Klopper could do."

The old man nodded, remembering the sound of the broomstick cracking through tiles on the hospital roof, the wind lifting the dirty white sheet, and silence as the gunfire had stopped. "We knew all that, but we were still ashamed . . . At first we could not believe we were prisoners of war. And then the shame . . . But my friend, Job, he was not going to sit around, feeling ashamed and doing nothing! Hhayi! He did *something*!"

John and Zanele glanced at each other.

"With just twenty little bullets, he sank a ship!"

The children grinned and nudged each other triumphantly, and Tabela gasped, having long forgotten her plan to slip away.

"The ship's cargo was petrol and ammunition for the German army in Greece. Job sank it. He blew it up. But we didn't ask him *how*, not then, not while we were still POWs. It was too dangerous to know . . . " The old man's voice had got a little hoarse and his speech was slower.

"Baba, you are tired now. Perhaps you should stop the story," MaGumede said anxiously.

"If these children are tired, I can stop," the old man said.

"No! No! We're fine," the children protested.

But Tabela stood up, stretching her stiff legs as she realised she'd spent the entire afternoon listening to her father's story. He was right, she thought to herself. He did have a story to tell. But he shouldn't go on any longer. Not with his dicey heart.

"MaGumede, I think I should take my father home for supper now," she said.

Outside the rain drummed steadily on the metal roof. MaGumede switched on a light.

"Perhaps you want to wait for the rain to stop. I have a pot of soup on the stove. Enough for us all," she said. "Hlala! Have something to eat first."

"OK. Thank you," Tabela decided. "And then I'll take him home."

John helped his grandmother set out bowls of steaming soup

and bread rolls. When they'd finished, Zanele opened the oven and took out an apricot tart. She sniffed it and sighed with pleasure.

"Pudding! Great!" John perked up. "So what happened to Job, Mr Ndebele?"

The old man took a spoonful of tart and savoured it slowly. He wiped his mouth and spoke again. "After the ship sank, Job disappeared with Samuel. Even after El Alamein, when the troops came back to free us, he was not with them . . . "

And his daughter, instead of taking him home, settled in to listen.

*

Every day they looked for Job, but he did not come back. They wondered if he were dead. All that time in the desert. But three weeks later an armoured car drove into the barracks and there was Job, with Samuel.

Sipho saw them go into Colonel Sayer's office and Colonel Smith joined them. Colonel Sayer was quite a good guy. He was OK. He was their commander, head of the Native Military Corps.

"NMC . . . That's what they called us African soldiers," Mr Ndebele explained.

The others nodded.

"When Job came out of Colonel Sayer's office, we asked him why he had escaped from the POW camp when he knew that the Allied army was winning at El Alamein, and we would soon be free. He said Franco had looked at him strangely, as if he knew something. He was worried about the military police.

"I remembered Franco looking strangely at Job, so I told him.

And then I said, 'That Franco, he could dance! His grandpa taught him the Greek dance.'

"That's when we understood. Franco's grandpa was Greek. The cargo on that ship was for the German army in Greece, probably fighting against Franco's family. Maybe Franco did know, but he'd kept quiet . . ."

Mr Ndebele gave himself a shake, remembering his indignation when Job told them Colonel Smith did not believe he had sunk a ship.

"Colonel Smith said it was not possible. But Colonel Sayer called Job again and asked him more questions. And then he asked all of us – Samuel, Andrew and Koos also – one at a time. I told him Job had collected fuse wire, a cigarette and matches, and twenty bullets. But that I didn't know what he'd done down in the hold.

"Colonel Sayer believed us because we told him those small things. Job and Samuel took Colonel Sayer to the hut and showed him the radio. They told him how they had listened to the BBC news. Job was so tired when he came back to the barracks, he went to sleep.

"Next day the officers took him to the harbour so he could show him where the ship had been – those guys still didn't believe him! At first the navy divers could not find the ship. But someone said maybe a tugboat pulled it out of the main shipping channel before it sank. They found the burnt ship under the water, and then they knew Job was speaking the truth."

John could not sit still. "Mr Ndebele, did the military police ever guess why the ship had exploded? Did they guess any of you had been involved?"

"No! Because when it exploded we were already back in camp, far from the harbour. So how could any of us have done it?"

"So Job *did* delay the explosion! Did he tell you how?"

Mr Ndebele nodded. "Now we were free. The Italians were gone, and it was safe for us to know. So he told us . . . "

21

A cigarette and matches

"This is it!" John whispered to Zanele.

In his quiet voice, Mr Ndebele spoke.

"Those things Job had found in the trenches – little bullets, fuse wire. He had taken the gunpowder out of the bullets and put it in a tin, and he had joined the pieces of fuse wire together to make a long piece. And the cigarette and some matches. He had them all in his jacket pocket while we were working on the ship. And when it was nearly time to leave the ship, he stayed down in the hold with the hatch closed.

"He opened some petrol drums and he splashed plenty of petrol around. Then he put the gunpowder near the spilt petrol and he covered it with straw. He did not hurry. With gunpowder you do not hurry. He knew his friends on deck would keep Franco busy and make enough time for him.

"He put one end of the fuse on top of the gunpowder. Then he zig-zagged the fuse wire backwards and forwards, and put the other end near the stairs. Fuse wire must be long. It was good fuse wire, the kind that burns slowly, and it was long, but not long enough! He knew we must all be far away from the harbour, back at the camp, before the fire reached the gunpowder. Even I knew the fuse was not long enough for that.

"But Job had a good plan, an excellent plan: he stood near the stairs and lit the cigarette. There was no filter on that cigarette. He stuck the fuse and four matches into the *other* end of the cigarette and left it to burn slowly. If you don't puff a cigarette it takes a long time to burn. Now there was enough time for Job to climb up the stairs, open the hatch and climb out. And enough time for us to get off the ship and get back to camp while the cigarette was burning slowly.

"When the fire in the cigarette reached the matches, they caught fire and lit the fuse wire. The fire ran along the fuse wire to the gunpowder. That little pile of gunpowder exploded. Then the spilt petrol caught alight. The open petrol drums exploded and the ammunition exploded, which sank the ship. Understand?" he asked the children, who nodded slowly.

"A smouldering cigarette!" John said thoughtfully. "So that was it. Lucky he didn't blow himself up. He lit a match down there, with petrol fumes, petrol drums and ammunition! If he'd got it wrong, you could all have been killed. And if he'd been caught, he'd have been shot."

Mr Ndebele nodded and the children were quiet as they imagined the petrol, gunpowder and fire in a ship's hold, and a military police firing squad. Enjoying the children's round-eyed amazement, the old man sat back in a glow of satisfaction.

But MaGumede was not convinced. She shook her head emphatically.

"That wouldn't have worked, Mkhulu! The cigarette would have gone out. My dressmaker smokes . . . "

John put his head in his hands. Here they were, hearing

about one of the greatest achievements by a single man in World War II, and his grandmother had to talk about her *dressmaker*?

"When my dressmaker takes pins out of a dress," MaGumede continued, "she puts them between her lips. But first she puts her cigarette in an ash tray, and it goes out. *Always!* And she has to relight it. It doesn't smoulder."

For a long while no one said a word.

Tabela's chair rasped on the floor. She stood up, jaw jutting.

"Hhayi wena! Hang on two minutes, everyone! Ima!" she said firmly and hurried out of the door, leaving behind an uncomfortable silence. How could Job's explanation not have been true? In less than two minutes Tabela was bustling back inside, shaking off rain drops. She settled herself into her chair.

"Here's a cigarette! From the father of those boys you played cricket with. See here! See what's written?"

They leant closer as she pointed at the tiny printing on the cigarette.

"*Reduced ignition propensity,*" she read. "Nowadays cigarettes are made like this, to go out if they are left, so they won't start a fire. But when you were young, Baba, cigarettes carried on burning."

She beamed at her father, who sighed with relief. Job had always told him the truth.

MaGumede nodded. "That makes sense," she conceded.

But Zanele was thinking of something else. "Mr Ndebele, why were Job and Samuel so long in the desert?"

The old man sat up a little straighter again.

"They were lost! For twenty-three days! Escaping was easy — they just dug holes in the sand and rolled out under the barbed wire in the dark. But finding their way in the desert was not so easy. They walked at night when it was cool. They walked too far south, and they missed our troops. Job had stored some food from the ship's galley and tins of milk and water bags, but it ran out. They told us that people on camels gave them dates to eat, and water. But later they thought they would die of thirst. That's when they saw a track in the sand, and soon a South African officer in an armoured car drove past. He brought Job and Samuel back to Tobruk."

By now Zanele could hardly contain herself. "Mr Ndebele, we saw Job yesterday! Job Maseko MM."

22

The light goes out

Old Mr Ndebele looked dazed, and the light that had animated his face as he'd told his story suddenly seemed to fade.

"I don't know what you're saying . . . " He turned to his daughter. "I must go home now, Tabela. How can these children say they saw him? He is not alive."

Zanele held her notebook open in front of him. "Here's why he got the Military Medal. The citation."

He read the first few words. "But then you already knew my story . . . " The old man slumped in his chair, feeling foolish. Why had he thought these children wanted to hear about these things?

John was dismayed at the old man's distress. "We did not know all of it, Mr Ndebele," John quickly reassured him. "We didn't know the last bit, the most important bit. And it was his *painting* that we saw," he explained. "His portrait. At the war museum in Joburg. The Museum of Military History."

The old man shook his head in wonder. "The painting of Job is there?"

Zanele beamed. "The painting was hidden away in a storeroom for fifty years, until 1994. Now it's hanging on the wall at the museum: Job Maseko MM. But for fifty years almost no one got to hear about him or what he did."

John pulled his phone out of his pocket and scrolled to the photo of the painting. "How's your eyesight, Mkhulu?"

Mr Ndebele looked at the photograph for several minutes before he spoke. "I watched a man painting this picture. We knew that painter's name, but I have forgotten."

"Neville Lewis," Zanele told him.

He nodded.

"The radio's also there, Mkhulu. Someone brought it back to South Africa," Zanele explained.

Tabela wiped a tear from the corner of her eye. "Baba, when Dumi brings the children back on Monday, we can ask him to take us to see the painting and the radio."

"I will like that. I would like to see my old friend, friend of my big brother, looking so proud, so strong. Major Sinclair and Colonel Sayer said Job Maseko should get the Victoria Cross. But it was that Colonel Smith who said it could not go to a native. Neville Lewis decided to paint Job's portrait anyway. In the war there were some great men, generous men. And plenty who were not."

"So there could have been five South African VCs," Zanele murmured.

"*Should* have been five!" John said decisively.

Everyone nodded in agreement and Mr Ndebele added, "We went to watch the artist, Neville Lewis, painting Job's portrait. And we heard Neville Lewis tell our Colonel Sayer that there was something splendid about Job Maseko, as if he had a light inside. 'I hope you can see that in my painting, in the eyes,' he told him.

And he was right about Job; he did seem to have a light inside. A glorious man. But when the letter came back from his fiancée, the light went out."

"His fiancée, Mkhulu? The other Zanele?" Zanele asked. "Do you know about the photos Job Maseko sent her? His beard had grown when he was a POW. He went to a photographer to take a photo of him with his beard, and then he shaved it off and went back for another photo. He sent both photos to his Zanele, to ask her which she preferred. I didn't find anything about her reply. Do you know?"

The old man sighed sadly. "Yes. Oh, yes. I know . . . She wrote to say she was going to marry someone else, so beard or no beard did not matter."

"She dumped him! A man like that!"

"I did not see Job smile after he got that letter. Before that, if any of us had trouble, he would make a plan. Even when we were POWs, he kept us smiling. But now we could not make *him* smile." Mr Ndebele was murmuring, as if to himself.

"And after the war," John interrupted, "back in South Africa, he didn't get the freedom he'd fought for. *You* didn't get it. Not for fifty years."

"No. We knew on the way home that things in South Africa would be just the same as before. When our ship was passing Madagascar, the sergeant major told us, 'It's time to get ready for the Union. Europeans queue here for their food. Non-Europeans queue there.' Job put his plate down and walked out of there. The sergeant major said he hoped Job wasn't going to become a troublemaker. And I thought how he'd sunk an enemy ship and won a medal because he was a troublemaker."

Mr Ndebele laughed bitterly.

"After Madagascar, we stood in separate queues again for food, for the first time since Rommel had come to the POW camp. So we knew we would not be getting freedom in South Africa. After the war, Smuts lost the elections and things got worse. Some men who had supported Hitler were in the government."

"So, Mkhulu," Zanele interrupted, "after the war, when you were back in South Africa, did you and Job work together again?"

"No, I didn't see Job again. Job went to Springs. I was a driver at a bank there in Krugersdorp, and I was fixing up an old car. When my car was ready, I thought I would drive it to show Job. But then I saw Andrew. Andrew told me he'd seen Job one night in front of the Joburg city hall. There were many thousands of people holding torches and listening to that famous fighter pilot, Sailor Malan. He was saying South Africa fought the war for freedom and we must not give up our freedom now!"

John gave Zanele a nudge and she nodded.

"Andrew said Job was standing on the edge of the crowd, just listening, and Job did not see him. When Andrew tried to get through the people, to find him, he was gone. It was the last time one of us saw our great friend. It was also Andrew who told me that Job had died . . . All my life I have been sorry I wasn't there to help Job, like he had always helped me! In 1994, when we were all, black and white, standing in the same queue to vote, I thought about Job and I wished –"

The children looked at him, waiting.

"How *did* he die, Mkhulu?" John prompted gently.

The old man hesitated. "Job joined the army for two things. To fight against Hitler so we could all be free, and to get money to pay lobola, so he could marry his Zanele. But he did not get Zanele. And he did not get freedom.

"In Tobruk he was called Lance Corporal Job Maseko MM. Back in South Africa he was called 'boy'. Job had thought South Africa would be different, and he said he could not live without the love of his life. They found a note after they found his body on the railway line . . . Not a good way for such a splendid man to die."

"Not like that!" Zanele whispered in dismay. "An accident?"

"No one knows for sure. No one saw."

The others stared silently at the old man for several minutes. Mr Ndebele patted Zanele's shoulder and got stiffly to his feet.

"Thank you, izingane zami, for listening to me. I am pleased I could tell this story before it's too late . . . And pleased to tell you too, Tabela."

His daughter nodded, a little shame-faced.

"I will be happy to see the painting and the radio in that museum," he added.

Outside, the rain had stopped. Mr Ndebele and his daughter said goodnight and went out into the cool summer evening. Resting a hand heavily on his daughter's shoulder and shuffling towards the gate, the old man looked up at the moonlit sky.

"And tomorrow will be a fine day for your cricket match," he said cheerfully.

23
The Abyssinian trout rod

It was a fine morning. John and Zanele had packed their bags and piled them just inside the front door when the two boys called out, "Come on, amaDurbs! Come and play soccer. Can you play soccer there in Durban? And a girl?" they asked laughing.

"Watch me!" Zanele said, dribbling the ball expertly between them.

When they were too hot from running they played cricket again. MaGumede came to sit at the gate to watch. John bowled a few easy leg breaks to the taller boy, and then he bowled a fast ball, but the batsman hit it hard and flat, right past John and up the road for four.

This guy can really bat, John thought. *I need to try something else.*

He bowled a slower ball, which seemed to be going wide but then turned in again. The batsman swiped at the ball and it slipped under the bat and hit the wicket.

"Howzat?" John shouted out. His grandmother clapped.

"Hey, Mehlo mane! That was a googly!" the tall boy grinned, half in admiration, half ruefully. "Now do it again!" he challenged.

John laughed. "Not sure I can!" he replied.

He made way for a car approaching slowly down the road.

"Here's my dad! We've got to go, guys! We're going back to Durban now, right after lunch! Thanks for the game," John said to the two boys, who picked up their soccer ball and casually said goodbye.

"How was it, Mama?" Musi asked his mother-in-law as he pulled in through the gate. "Is your house still in one piece? I was worried when I heard the weather forecast. How'd you cope with them in the rain?"

"I had help."

When he raised his eyebrows she added, "My old neighbour entertained them. Zanele will tell you." She went into her kitchen and brought out a tray of glasses and a jug of her icy homemade lemonade.

"Lunch under the grapevine again!" she called, and flicked away a cloth covering the lunch platters on the table.

"Coronation chicken!" John said.

His grandmother laughed. "Otherwise known as leftover curry with yoghurt."

"So, Zanele," their father coaxed as they settled in around the table, "tell me how an old man kept my unruly children out of trouble."

Zanele and John starting speaking together.

"One at a time! Please!" Musi said, laughing. Were these the same jaded teenagers he'd left just a day ago?

"OK, Zanele, you tell. It's *your* story," said John.

"Dad, at the war museum we saw a painting of a black soldier who won a medal in the Second World War 'cos he sank a ship! I've started writing about it. And d'you *know*, Gogo's old neighbour, Mr Ndebele, was actually there! He told us all about it," she said without stopping to breathe.

"I knew *nothing* about black South Africans in the war until Jo told us about the man who drove with her dad," Musi replied. "But it's great that you've got it, Zanele!"

"Got what?"

"A true story!"

*

When lunch was done, Tabela opened the gate and she and her father came slowly up the path.

"I want to say goodbye to these children," the old man said.

"Thlala, Baba. Thlala, Tabela, sit!" MaGumede told them. She introduced them to Musi, who handed out glasses of lemonade.

"He only woke at lunch time," Tabela whispered to MaGumede. "But he seems a bit better now."

John had brought their suitcases outside, ready to be packed into the car. Now he opened a narrow canvas bag and took out pieces of the old trout rod.

"Mr Ndebele, one last thing. This trout rod belongs to my friend, Ted Punnett. Ted's great-grandpa used this rod in Abyssinia, during the war, so he and his driver could have a break from tinned food."

The old man took the two pieces from John, fitted them together and stood up. He stepped out onto the paving a bit unsteadily. They all watched as he planted his feet wide apart and drew the rod back to one side. He flicked it expertly as if casting, and watched as if to see where the line would land. The old man let out a delighted laugh.

Then he staggered a little, and John helped him sit down.

"I can still cast! I caught trout in Abyssinia," he told them. "The captain had a rod like this. One day we stopped next to a waterfall and the captain said he was going to catch rainbows. I thought he wasn't right in the head." He chuckled. "He caught fish! Rainbow-coloured trout. We'd eat them for supper." He paused, remembering. "He showed me how to cast the line so that it floats gently in the air across the water. There was a fly on the hook instead of bait. Connemara Black, he called that fly: 'Try this Connemara Black.' That first day, I caught the supper. He said not many people can catch a trout first time."

John scrummaged in his bag and pulled out a flat, square tin. He opened it with a flourish, pointing to a little hook with short black hairs tied to it.

"This fly?"

The old man nodded. "Just like that. And sometimes I used that one, Invicta."

His eyes became unfocused as he thought of something else.

"Often the nights were cool in the mountains, and there was mist, but one time it was too hot, a hot wind blowing. We slept with our tents open, and a fire was in between the tents to keep away lions.

"Late in the night something woke me. I put my head out to look. The fire was nearly out, and there was an animal, dark like a shadow in the moonlight, and big. Going inside the Captain's tent. Often I was afraid, but that night there was no time. I picked up a stick, still red from the fire, and I shouted, and I hit the animal. It turned and ran out and up the mountain. The captain told me he was dreaming that someone was snoring near him but when I shouted he woke up and saw the hyena's teeth right over his face. He always said I saved his life."

Zanele raised a questioning eyebrow at her dad and at John, who smiled and gave a little nod. She whispered to John, "You already knew?"

"I've been wondering," he replied. "Mkhulu, what was the captain's name?"

"I don't remember his name. Just the nickname: Fluff."

No one spoke. The old man looked at each of the children, puzzled.

"Mkhulu," John said, "in Joburg we stayed with Jo Punnett. Her dad's nickname was Fluff. He went with a driver – the best driver, he said – into the Abyssinian mountains to look for an alternative route in case the pass was blocked. Was that *you*?"

The old man's face broke into a slow, surprised smile.

"He tried to find you after the war, Mkhulu! He wrote to the mine, but they didn't have an address," John told him.

"I did not go to that mine again because I could drive! Yo! So that captain was Jo's father! He and I had many adventures. One day we were driving across the river, not too deep –"

"And your lorry got stuck on a rock?"

The old man laughed. "Hhayi wena! You know all my stories! That time in the flood we were lucky! And the Askaris didn't catch us there . . . " He gave a loud snort. "But the Italians, they nearly caught us. We were driving to join our army and in front was dust from twenty, thirty lorries. The sun was shining through the dust so we could not see well." Mr Ndebele became animated. "'Put your foot down, Lance Corporal! Let's join the convoy,' the captain said. So I drove fast. But when we were already close to the convoy, we could see those were Italian lorries. Maybe they had seen us, maybe there was too much dust. Then the road made a fork. The Italian lorries went left, so I drove quickly right. The captain laughed. He said, 'That was a close call! Quick thinking!'"

They smiled as Mr Ndebele continued.

"We South Africans chased away that Italian army in East Africa. We won that part of the war. Our army and air force with soldiers from Kenya, Nigeria, England. Then I went to Tobruk and the captain stayed there."

"Mkhulu, Jo Punnett's dad told her you had 'true grit'," John said.

He smiled dismissively. "I was too often afraid."

John slid the pieces of trout rod into the bag. "Mama Tabela," he said, "the captain, Fluff, couldn't thank Mr Ndebele, but his daughter might want to. Jo Punnett. When you go to Saxonwold . . . "

"Perhaps we can all go together," Gogo Gumede suggested.

"Mkhulu," Zanele turned to the old man, "I've written a copy of Job Maseko's citation for you. His name's misspelt – it's not *Masego*. Would you like it?"

The old man nodded and took the paper on which she'd written:

The King has been graciously pleased to approve the following award in recognition of gallant and distinguished service in the Middle East:
MILITARY MEDAL
No N 4448 L/Cpl Job Masego – Native Military Corps
CITATION
For meritorious and courageous action in that on or about the

21st July, while a Prisoner-of-war, he, Job Masego, sank a fully laden enemy steamer – probably an "F" boat – while moored in Tobruk Harbour.

This he did by placing a small tin filled with gunpowder in among drums of petrol in the hold, leading a fuse therefrom to the hatch and lighting the fuse upon closing the hatch.

In carrying out this deliberately planned action, Job Masego displayed ingenuity, determination and complete disregard of personal safety from punishment by the enemy or from the ensuing explosion which set the vessel alight.

"So there should have been five South African VCs," Zanele said emphatically, as Mr Ndebele tucked it into his shirt pocket.

"Zanele, mntanami, I saw you writing in your notebook." He was a bit breathless. "I will be pleased if you write this story."

"I'm on to it, Mkhulu." Zanele gripped her notebook tightly.

Tabela had been quiet but now she cleared her throat. "Baba, you have told us about that great man, Job Maseko. You must also tell your great-grandchildren that story, even though they are little. They must hear it from you. And *I* will tell them about our own hero, who fought a hyena to save another man's life."

Musi Matshoba stood up and stretched. "We must get back to Durban. Thank you for entertaining them yesterday, Mr Ndebele. Thank you too, Mama Tabela. I knew they'd have a good time here, Mama!"

MaGumede laughed. "That's more than I knew."

As Zanele looked around at her grandmother's house again, she asked suddenly, "Gogo, where did you live before here?"

"Near Mbombelo."

"Not in Soweto? So when did you come here? How did you get here?"

"Come on, Zanele," her father said impatiently.

"Off you go! Hamba! I'll tell you about it in Durban. I was eighteen. I walked."

So Gogo *does* have a story, Zanele thought, delighted.

John climbed into the car and stuck his head out of the passenger window. "It was really cool, Gogo!" he called out. "Thank you. We'll be back!"

From the back seat, Zanele looked at him with raised eyebrows. "Wasn't listening to an old madala supposed to be your 'worst nightmare'?"

He gave a crooked grin. "Don't forget the omagriza! OK, so I was wrong. Who'd have thought?"

The soccer players moved to the side of the road as Musi drove out of the gate.

"Watch it, Four Eyes! I'll get *you* out with a googly next time!" the tall boy called after them.

As they turned onto the road to the hospital, Zanele looked through the back window at the three little figures in the distance.

"He seemed to use all his strength telling us his story," she murmured, watching Mr Ndebele shuffle through her gogo's gate, leaning heavily on Tabela's shoulder. "D'you think we'll see him again?"

John was thoughtful.

"I think we met him just in time."

The end

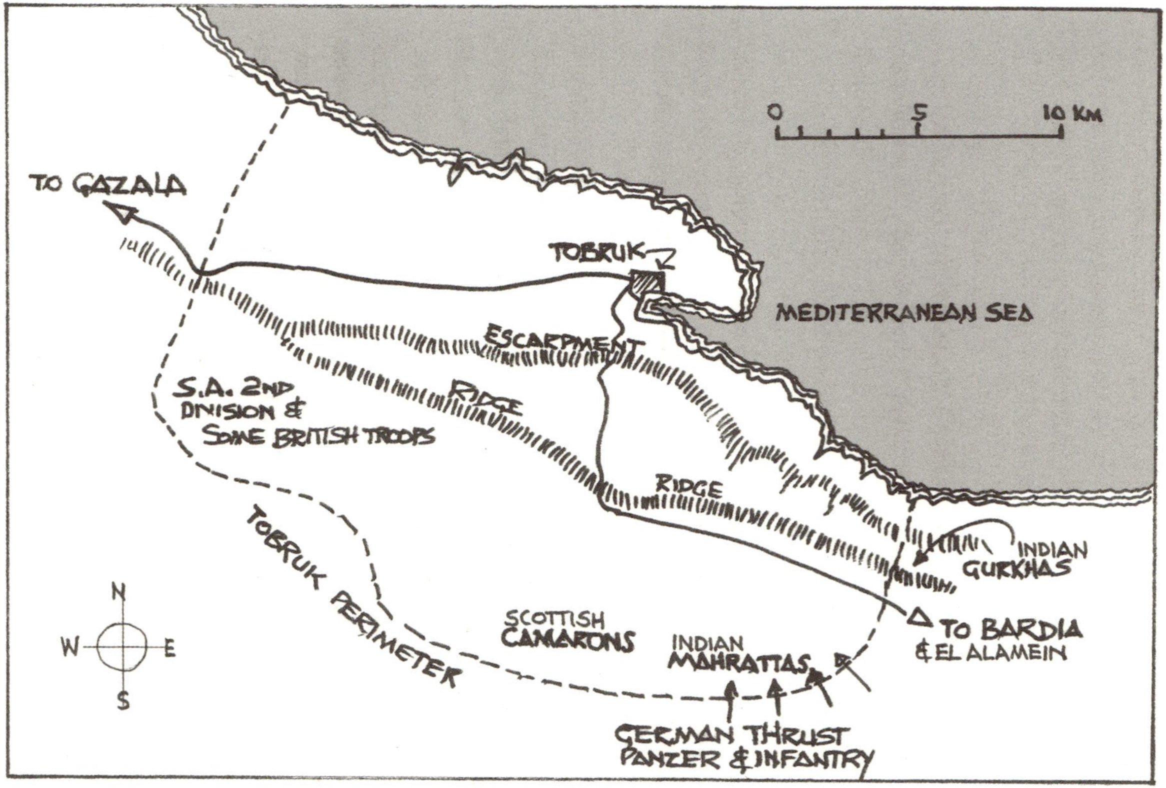

TOBRUK – JUNE 20TH 1942 – TROOP POSITIONS

Author's notes

Job Maseko MM

You can see the painting of Job Maseko by war artist Neville Lewis, as well as the radio brought from Tobruk, in the Ditsong: National Museum of Military History in Saxonwold, Johannesburg.

Although official South Africa forgot about Job Maseko for fifty years, some World War II veterans' organisations did not. People from old soldiers' organisations such as Sailor Malan's Springbok Legion, the Moths (Memorable Order of Tin Hats) and the Sappers (the army engineers) joined the Maseko family when they consecrated a stone at Job's grave in 1976.

Years later, a film director named Vincent Moloi heard mention of Job Maseko on the radio. He visited the Museum of Military History, where he found Job Maseko's portrait and decided to make a film about Job. Job's sister was still alive at the time, and when Moloi visited her she told him about her big brother, Job, and his fiancée, Zanele, and how Job died.

Moloi found other people who had known Job or who, like Job, had fought in the desert, including some who had been prisoners of war. With Moloi's permission, I have used some of their actual words from the movie he directed and from translations of the uncut interviews. They described the many hundreds of planes flying over Tobruk "like a swarm of locusts". They spoke of the terror of facing heavily armed German soldiers when they were unarmed. And they spoke of what the returning black soldiers were told as their ship passed Madagascar.

Vincent Moloi's film is called *A Pair of Boots and a Bicycle* (2007). Moloi wrote that he made this film celebrating Job Maseko's bravery because, as he put it, "our mothers and fathers were denied the opportunity to know their history".

The book *The Unknown Force: Black, Indian and Coloured Forces Through Two World Wars*, by Ian Gleeson, shows a picture of Major General FH Theron presenting the Military Medal to Job Maseko. The book also has a photograph of the radio that is now in the museum.

The information in the paragraph below comes from Ian Gleeson's book. It is reproduced here with his permission:

Job Maseko joined the Native Military Corps early in 1942.

He was attached to the 2nd Infantry Division and was promoted to Lance Corporal.

Job Maseko died in 1952 and was buried in the Payneville Township Cemetery in Springs.

The township of KwaThema near Springs has a primary school named after him.

The main road linking Springs to KwaThema, as well as a South African Navy fast attack craft, are also named after him.

Gleeson's book also tells us that the friends who distracted the Italian guard while Job Maseko was in the hold were Andrew Mohudi, Samuel Masiya, another man called Sam (last name unlisted) and Jacob Skawe, all from a regiment called the Native Military Corps, as well as Koos Willem and a Private Roelf from the Cape Corps.

Job Maseko receiving the Military Medal

What is fact and what is fiction?

The account of Job Maseko's actions and how he delayed the explosion comes from what he told the war artist Neville Lewis and Colonel Sayer. Colonel Sayer later wrote about it in a book called *Sabotage at Tobruk, Leaves from a Soldier's Notebook*.

Job Maseko *did* encourage his fellow POWs to continue fighting the Nazis and fascists by sabotaging enemy lorries and machinery.

Some books and websites say Job Maseko worked at an explosives factory before the war. Some say he was a delivery man and some say he worked on a mine. In this story I have assumed these could all be correct – but I have no evidence that he worked as a translator.

I have gleaned a few facts about Job Maseko's childhood from phrases spoken by his much younger sister (in an interview with Vincent Moloi) and information given me by the deputy principal of the Job Maseko Primary School. I have created the childhood character of Job based on those few facts, but the anecdotes of his childhood are fictional. Job's sister spoke of her big brother taking her to visit their grandparents' farm when she was a little girl, but I could not establish where this was. She spoke of Job with warmth, and her words suggest that Job was a kind and thoughtful big brother who might have cast a brotherly eye on Sipho, the fictional young brother of his fictional friend, Mzi.

When the Allied army surrendered at Tobruk, two British officers drove around waving a tiny, and not very visible, white flag. Two black South African soldiers climbed up on to the roof of the army headquarters and hoisted a white sheet which was seen for miles around. That is fact, but I could not find their names. Neither could I find the name of the black POW who welcomed the triumphantly returning Allied soldiers with a white flag, so in this book Sipho was given both these tasks.

The words ascribed to both General Rommel and General Klopper are their actual words.

The information about black soldiers being armed with .303 Lee Enfield rifles before the battle of El Alamein comes from the interview Vincent Moloi held with Private Petrus Dlamini, who was a veteran of El Alamein and who was given one of these guns and trained to use it. He said they were armed at the insistence of British and Australian officers. It seems no mention of this was made in despatches to South Africa.

Black veterans also spoke about what was said as their ship passed Madagascar on the return voyage. They were told to "practise for when they were back in the Union", meaning that black and white troops had to again queue separately for meals.

I have no record of the BBC broadcast after the battle of El Alamein. Using the record of events at El Alamein, I have guessed what may have been said.

Sipho Ndebele, based on a real-life hero

When I visited the war museum in Johannesburg and saw the portrait of Job Maseko and heard his story, my first reaction was, "I didn't know there were black South African soldiers in World War II." I had shared the collective amnesia that Vincent Moloi referred to.

But then a memory, long buried, floated up from my childhood: my father responding to my big brother's request for a story. "What did you do in the war, Daddy?"

My father did not mention fighting. He told us, instead, about his adventures. I remember him telling us about the very young black South African who was with him while they were scouting for an alternative route through the Abyssinian mountains.

He told us about the suicide pills, the encounter with the lion, their lorry being stuck in a flooded river, trout fishing in mountains streams and about him being saved from a hyena by this young man.

My father said, "He was very young, and very frightened, and very brave! When it mattered, he came up to scratch. That's true grit!"

After the war my father wrote to him at the mine where he had worked before the war, but the letter was returned: Address unknown. I have used what I know of this brave man to create the character of Lance Corporal Sipho Ndebele, through whose eyes much of this story is told.

General Smuts's promise: The Atlantic Charter

The Allied countries were fighting against Nazism and fascism, but what were they fighting *for?* In August 1941, the president of the United States, Franklin D Roosevelt, wrote a list of eight principles, which he asked the Allied countries to sign. These were principles on which they could base their hopes for a better world after the war. The principles included the right of all nations to self-determination and the right of all people to live in freedom.

It was called the Atlantic Charter and it was signed by Sir Winston Churchill and leaders of the other Allied countries.

The Star newspaper reported General Jan Smuts endorsing the principles of the Atlantic Charter when he read them to new army recruits in September 1941.

Many black South Africans volunteered to fight for the principles of the Atlantic Charter. But the Atlantic Charter was not honoured by the USA, Britain or South Africa until many years later. In the United States, many black people in the Southern States were not able to vote until the late 1960s. Great Britain did not give independence to her colonies until the 1960s (except, reluctantly and after much bloodshed, to India in 1947, and to Ghana in 1957). South Africa achieved democratic freedom for members of all races in 1994.

Neville Lewis, war artist

While Neville Lewis was painting Job Maseko's portrait, the two men talked, and so Lewis heard more details of events in the ship's hold than the officers did. Job told Lewis, who then told Colonel Sayer, how he had compensated for the shortness of the fuse by using a lit cigarette.

Besides painting a portrait of Lance Corporal Job Maseko, Lewis painted many war heroes including Field Marshall Lord Montgomery of El Alamein, Field Marshal Jan Smuts, Major General Dan Pienaar and Private Lucas Majosi DCM, also of El Alamein. After the war he lived in South Africa, where he painted Chief Albert Luthuli in the 1950s.

Neville Lewis had studied painting at the Slade School of Fine Art at the University of London, England, under Henry

Tonks, one of the most famous war artists of all time. Tonks was a surgeon and an artist, whose work was used by the first plastic surgeons when they reconstructed soldiers' damaged faces.

Neville Lewis's paintings of soldiers from South Africa's various armed forces – airmen, sailors, soldiers, as well as nurses – were used on postage stamps during the war. Below is a painting of a member of the Native Military Corps. It was the only one of these paintings not used on a stamp. He thought it was the best.

Another painting by Neville Lewis

Sailor Malan was called "the best pilot of the war"

Adolph 'Sailor' Malan
Group Captain Adolph Gysbert Malan,
DSO & Bar, DFC & Bar

Sailor Malan joined the RAF in Britain before the war because, when he was a sailor with Safmarine and his ship had visited Germany, he had seen what the Nazis were doing and guessed they were hoping to dominate the world. He led RAF Squadron No. 74 during the height of the Battle of Britain, and trained dozens of pilots. He developed a set of simple rules for fighter pilots, to be handed to everyone in the RAF Fighter Command. Tacked to the wall of most airbases was his: 'TEN OF MY RULES FOR AIR FIGHTING'.

Air Commodore Alan Deere wrote of him: "Sailor Malan was the best pilot of the war; a good tactician, an above average pilot and an excellent shot" (see www.historylearningsite.co.uk).

In an essay on Sailor Malan, Bill Nasson, wrote, "Air Chief Marshal Sir Hugh Dowding, not given to gushing compliments, said he was 'one of the great assets of the Command – a fighter pilot who was not solely concerned with his own score, but as one whose first thoughts were for the efficiency of his squadron and the personal safety of his junior pilots'."

After the war Sailor Malan worked with the anti-apartheid-groups, the Torch Commando and the Springbok Legion. Springbok Legion members met with Oliver Tambo and Walter Sisulu in 1955.

Did General Klopper mess up at Tobruk?

Before 1942, South Africa's General Klopper had been a staff officer, working at a desk, for most of the war. He knew almost nothing about leading an army. He had fought bravely in the field for just a few months before he was made general on 14 May 1942, and was sent to Tobruk to command thirty-three thousand men from several different countries.

When he arrived in Tobruk, he found the defences had not been maintained. He did not repair the defences because he was told by General Auchinleck to, "Prepare to evacuate Tobruk ahead of Rommel's advance." Klopper obeyed orders and instructed the army to move supplies out of Tobruk.

The Allies knew Rommel was advancing across the desert with the German Afrika Korps, the Italian army and with new Panzer tanks. But they did not know how fast Rommel was coming because the Chief of Intelligence had already left Tobruk, taking his reconnaissance planes with him.

On 15 June 1942, General Klopper's orders were changed. He was given a message that came from British Prime Minister Winston Churchill: "Stay and defend Tobruk."

Klopper again obeyed orders. He and thirty-three thousand troops stayed in Tobruk and four days later, on June 19, Rommel attacked.

If you are wondering why, just four days before Rommel and his Afrika Korps reached Tobruk, Prime Minister Winston Churchill gave that strange order, you can read Churchill's explanation in his book, *The Second World War, Volume IV*. Churchill wrote:

We did not know the conditions prevailing in Tobruk. It was inconceivable that the already well proved fortifications of Tobruk should not have been maintained in the highest efficiency, and indeed strengthened.

Unbeknown to me... General Auchinleck had issued instructions [to General Klopper] that if we were forced to withdraw 'it is not my intention to hold on to it [Tobruk] once the enemy is in a position to invest it effectively. Should this appear inevitable, the place will be evacuated and the maximum amount of destruction carried out in it.'

In consequence of these orders the defences had not been maintained in good shape. Many mines had been lifted for use elsewhere, gaps had been driven through the wire for the passage of vehicles, and the sand had silted up much of the anti-tank ditch so that in places it was hardly an obstacle...

At home we had no inkling that the evacuation of Tobruk had ever entered into the plans or thoughts of the commanders [Ritchie and Auchinleck].

So, on 15 June, Churchill sent his order in a telegram to General Auchinleck because he was worried that Auchinleck's orders '*did not positively require him* [General Klopper] *to defend Tobruk*'. Churchill wrote in the telegram: *We are glad to have your assurance that you have no intention of giving up Tobruk.*

It was at that point that General Klopper was instructed not to withdraw from Tobruk. But Generals Auchinleck and Ritchie seem not to have communicated with the air force about the change of plan:

On June 19, the day of Rommel's attack, all fighter pilots from the combined RAF, SAAF and other Allied air forces were given seven days' leave and they all, except two, left the airbase and went to Cairo. Bomber pilots were put on a 3-day leave rota.
(From James Ambrose Brown, *Eagles Strike*)

Churchill's words about this were: "*No fighter* [plane] *protection could be given to our troops as our Air Force was withdrawn to distant landing grounds.*" In his book *War in the Desert*, Neil Orpen agrees, saying: "Tobruk was the only battle fought in the Western Desert where the Allied 8th Army did not have full support from the air force."

In contrast, on the same day, 19 June, the German forces had every available Luftwaffe and Italian Air Force bomber unit in North Africa and every available dive bomber from Greece and Crete ready on a landing ground just eight miles from Tobruk.

In his book, *Jan Smuts by his Son*, JC Smuts makes it clear that Jan Smuts knew Churchill was partly to blame for the fall of Tobruk, but Smuts chose not to point a finger at Churchill. Instead, General Klopper (and South Africa) carried most of the blame and the shame, and Churchill, who was inspiring the Allies to victory, was not discredited.

A few months after the fall of Tobruk, Churchill transferred Auchinleck and Ritchie, and soon afterwards General Montgomery took over. Churchill spread the blame when he later wrote: "*I am sure we were headed for disaster under the former regime* [meaning Generals Auchinleck and Ritchie]. *The army was oppressed by a sense of bafflement and uncertainty.*"

Reports vary on the number of men taken prisoner at Tobruk.

Neil Orpen uses the figure thirty-three thousand, and then twenty-four thousand on the same page. There were certainly thirty-three thousand men in Tobruk on 19 June. Some were killed and some escaped before General Klopper surrendered. I have surmised that twenty-four thousand prisoners of war were taken when Tobruk fell, and more were rounded up later.

The Victoria Cross

The four South Africans who were awarded the Victoria Cross were Edwin Swales VC (a bomber pilot who died in the course of his action and is widely acknowledged to be one of the bravest of all recipients of the Victoria Cross), Gerard Norton VC, Quentin Smythe VC and John Nettleton VC. Google their citations and decide if John and Zanele were right: Job Maseko should have received the Victoria Cross.

Acknowledgements and thanks

Because I cannot possibly know what it was like to be a young African boy in the 1930s growing up in the country, far from any town, I used Oliver Tambo's description of his childhood, as he narrated it to Luli Callinicos for her biography, *Oliver Tambo: Beyond the Engeli Mountains*. Oliver Tambo described the attitudes of his father's friends to school education and to letter-writing. In one instance I use his actual words: when Sipho's father wonders if a letter will "come back".

And because I cannot know what it was like to be a prisoner of war, I referred to Hillie Feldman's memoir of his time as a prisoner of war in the Western Desert, and to Karen Horn's interviews with prisoners of war. I took the anecdote about the dejected commanding officer and the dog from Horn's PHD thesis, *Narratives from North Africa: South African Prisoner-of-war experience following the fall of Tobruk, June 1942*.

From another of Callinicos's books, *A Place in the City: the Rand on the Eve of Apartheid*, I learnt of the cattle disease that followed the terrible drought years of the 1930s, which drove so many people, of all races, to the cities.

Callinicos put me in touch with Vincent Moloi and Edwin Wes, who were very generous with their help. They gave me a copy of their documentary film about Job Maseko, *A Pair of Boots and a Bicycle*, and sent me the unabridged transcripts of interviews with Job Maseko's sister and with black war veterans. With their permission I have on occasion put words from these interviews into the mouths of characters in this book. The description of the bombing of Tobruk is an example.

The war veterans interviewed for the documentary, and whose words I have used, were Sgt Freddie Nkoma, Sgt Charles Adams, Cpl John Currie, Pvt Rammos Mautsoa, Pvt Petrus Dlamini, Pvt John Magnus Africa and Pvt Lota Mfelang.

My family and friends recalled my father's anecdotes. Peter Strauss remembered my father speaking of his relief that he had not had to shoot the lion in Abyssinia "because it wasn't hungry". My brother, Clive, remembered our father's story of the Italian convoy. Our father told us about Sailor Malan, The Torch Commando and the Springbok Legion, of which our father was a member.

I am grateful to the people who helped me with isiZulu words and phrases: Tom Nkosi, publisher of *Ziwaphi*, and his staff; Pitso Mosethle, publisher of *Metro News*, and his young staff, who suggested the modern, slangy and disrespectful phrases about old people that infuriated Zanele; Dorothy Wheeler and the staff of the Johannesburg Bar Council Library and Archives. Thumeke Nyilika suggested isiZulu words and phrases, and Sabelo Ntozinzima, who has a small farm, told me about raising calves and about stick fighting.

The staff of the Ditsong South African Museum of Military History gave their time generously. They scanned and sent the photographs. Thank you to Ilze Cloete, Alan Sinclair, Caroline Johnson, Kenneth Madia and Elizabeth Mnguni, Hamish Paterson, the archivist, and John King, the managing director.

Henrietta Dax allowed me to use Clarke's Bookshop's wonderful collection of military history books as a library. Thank you.

I am grateful to the people who lent me books: Mike Prothero lent me the books about Rommel that are listed below; Ronnie Kasrils lent me *The Unknown Force: Black, Indian and Coloured Soldiers Through Two World Wars* by Ian Gleeson; Martin Bramwell lent me Joel Mervis's book, *South Africa in World War II*; and Richard Weeks lent me *Justice Misfired* by Gordon Bamford, about a miner.

The only available photograph of black WWII POWs was not suitable for a cover design, so we staged a photograph. When Captain Francois Morkel of the Cape Town Castle heard we needed uniforms and paraphernalia for the photo shoot, he swung into action, hunted through the museum's storerooms and found the various uniforms worn by the three actors in the cover photograph. The CEO of the Cape Town Castle, Calvin Gilfillan, and Derek Williams and Sergeant Major Plaaitjies, were also very helpful.

I am very grateful to Josie Borain, who took the dramatic cover photograph, to Nadene Kriel, who directed the shoot and designed the cover, and to the three actors: Charles Siboto, Hugo Tanda and David Omari.

Dr Marcia Leveson and Barbara Ludman checked early drafts of the manuscript. Thank you. And my thanks to the people who read all or some of the manuscript, in its various forms, and encouraged me: Dr Carole Silver, who died in January 2015; my sister, Claire Fanarof; Joan Kruger; Dr Karen Horn; Rose Zwi; Richard Honikman; Luli Callinicos; Dr Selma Brode and Jules Brode (a WWII veteran); Eve Grey; Rheina Epstein; Ingrid Mennen; my sons, Langley, Tom and Nick Kirkwood; all my grandchildren and my great-nephew, Ben Leveson.

Jay Heale read two early drafts and quite rightly rejected both, with very helpful criticism. My husband, Richard Honikman, drew the maps. Thank you.

Tafelberg Publishers do things well. Thank you to my publisher, Michelle Cooper, and to Nicky Stubbs, the marketing manager, who believed in this manuscript. Michelle put it into the hands of an inspired editor, Nicola Rijsdijk. I was thrilled with the editing, which was meticulous, creative and sensitive.

Dr Karen Horn checked the manuscript for historical accuracy. I added to the manuscript after she read it. If there are errors, the fault is mine, not hers.

Dumisani Sibiya edited the isiZulu words and phrases. Thank you.

References

BOOKS, ARTICLES AND LETTERS:

Birkby, C, *Dancing the Skies*
   Cape Town: Howard Timmins Publishers, 1982
Bowyer, C & Shores, C, *Desert Air Force War*
   London: Ian Allen, 1981
Brown, JA, *Eagles Strike: The campaigns of the South African Air Force in Egypt, Cyrenaica, Libya, Tunisia, Tripolitania and Madagascar 1941-1943*
   Johannesburg: Purnell, 1974

Callinicos, L, *Gold and Workers: A People's History of South Africa Volume One*
   Johannesburg: Ravan Press, 1980
Callinicos, L, *A Place in the City: The Rand on the Eve of Apartheid*
   Johannesburg: Ravan Press, 1993
Callinicos, L, *Oliver Tambo: Beyond the Engeli Mountains*
   Cape Town: David Philip, 2004
Chetty, S, "Imagining National Unity: South African propaganda efforts during the Second World War"
   Kronos, Vol 38 No 1, 2012
Churchill, WS, *The Second World War Volume IV: The Hinge of Fate*
   London: Cassell & Co, 1949

Feldman, H, *World War Two and Me (1939 to 1945)*
   Private memoir of a South African POW captured in the Western Desert

Giliomee, H & Mbenga, B, *New History of South Africa*
   Cape Town: Tafelberg, 2007

Gleeson, I, *The Unknown Force: Black, Indian and Coloured Soldiers Through Two World Wars*
   Rivonia: Ashanti Publishers, 1994
Grundlingh, LWF, *The Participation of South African Blacks in the Second World War*
   D Phill, D Litt thesis, 1986

Killingray, D & Rathbone, R (eds), *Africa and the Second World War*,
   Chapter by Grundlingh LWF
   London: Palgrave and Macmillan, 1986

Horn, K, "Narratives from North Africa: South African prisoner-of-war experiences following the fall of Tobruk, June 1942"
   Historia, Vol 56 No 2, 2011

Katz, D, "The Greatest Military Reversal of South African Arms: The Fall of Tobruk 1942, an avoidable blunder or an inevitable disaster?"
   (www.academia.edu/2644030)

Lande, DA, *Rommel in North Africa*
   Osceola, USA: MBI Publishing Company, 1999
Liddell, BH (ed), *The Rommel Papers*
   London: Harper Collins, 1953

"Maseko" archival record
   Union War Histories (UWH), Box 128,
   South African National Defence Force Archives
Mendelowitz, B, *Forgotten Hero: The story of Job Maseko*
   Johannesburg: Sached Books, 1997
   (Excerpt in *Drum* magazine, March 2000)
Mervis, J, *South Africa in World War II*
   Johannesburg: Times Media, 1989
Mitcham, SW, Jr, *Rommel's Greatest Victory: The Desert Fox and the Fall of Tobruk*
   Navoto Ca.: Presidio Press, 1998
Mohlamme, JS, "Soldiers Without Reward: Africans in South Africa's Wars" (review)
   Military History Journal, Vol 10 No 1, June 1995

Nasson, B, "A flying Springbok of wartime British skies:
AG 'Sailor' Malan"
Kronos, Vol 35 No 1, 2009

Orpen, ND, *War in the Desert*
Johannesburg: Purnell, 1971

Sayer, HO, *Sabotage at Tobruk: Leaves from a soldier's notebook*
Dep. Dir. Of Non-European Army Services
(Found on the internet)

Smuts, JC, *Jan Christian Smuts by his son*
Cape Town: Heinemann and Cassell, 1952

Time-Life Books, *The Southern Front (The Third Reich)*
Alexandria, Virginia: Time-Life Education, 1950

Woods, D, Interview with Job Masego [sic])
Cape Times, 8 March 1976

Young, D, *Rommel*
London: Fontana Books, 1950
(Desmond Young served under General Auchinleck)

A wartime letter written by Jenny Hobbs' uncle and kindly supplied by her.

DOCUMENTARY FILM:

A Pair of Boots and a Bicycle
2007, (d/Vincent Moloi, p/Edwin Wes)
Including translations of the unabridged interviews that were done during the making of the film.